THE SIERRA FORAGER

THE SIERRA FORAGER

YOUR GUIDE TO WILD EDIBLE PLANTS OF THE TAHOE, YOSEMITE, AND MAMMOTH REGIONS

MIA ANDLER

Heyday, Berkeley, California

Disclaimer about Dangers of Wild Edibles

Eating wild plants can be dangerous or even deadly. Please do not harvest anything you cannot identify with absolute certainty. The author and publishers of this book are not responsible for your choices or the consequences of your eating wild edible plants.

Library of Congress Cataloging-in-Publication Data

Names: Andler, Mia, author.
Title: The Sierra forager: your guide to edible wild plants of the Tahoe, Yosemite, and Mammoth regions / Mia Andler.
Other titles: Your guide to edible wild plants of the Tahoe, Yosemite, and Mammoth regions
Description: Berkeley, California : Heyday, [2023] | Includes index.
Identifiers: LCCN 2022026987 (print) | LCCN 2022026988 (ebook) | ISBN 9781597145947 (paperback) | ISBN 9781597145954 (epub)
Subjects: LCSH: Wild plants, Edible—Sierra Nevada (Calif. and Nev.) | Field guides.
Classification: LCC QK98.5.S54 A54 2023 (print) | LCC QK98.5.S54 (ebook) | DDC 581.6/32097944—dc23/eng/20220629
LC record available at https://lccn.loc.gov/2022026987
LC ebook record available at https://lccn.loc.gov/2022026988

Cover Art: MoreVectors/Shutterstock
Cover and Interior Design: Debbie Berne

Additional photo credits
page 10: Map by David Deis; page 11: Mieszko9/Shutterstock; page 98: Madeleine Steinbach / Shutterstock; page 115: Wirestock Creators / Shutterstock (bottom right); Jhor Hyozdetsky / Shutterstock (bottom left); page 121: Raja Sopan Purbo / Shutterstock; page 142: DNB STOCK / Shutterstock; pages 154, 172, 178: Stephen Sharnoff

Published by Heyday
P.O. Box 9145, Berkeley, California 94709
(510) 549-3564
heydaybooks.com

Printed in East Peoria, Illinois, by Versa Press, Inc.

10 9 8 7 6 5 4 3 2 1

FSC
www.fsc.org
MIX
Paper from
responsible sources
FSC® C005010

To the life-giving waters of the High Sierra
and the plants you nurture.
May you be pure and abundant
for future generations.

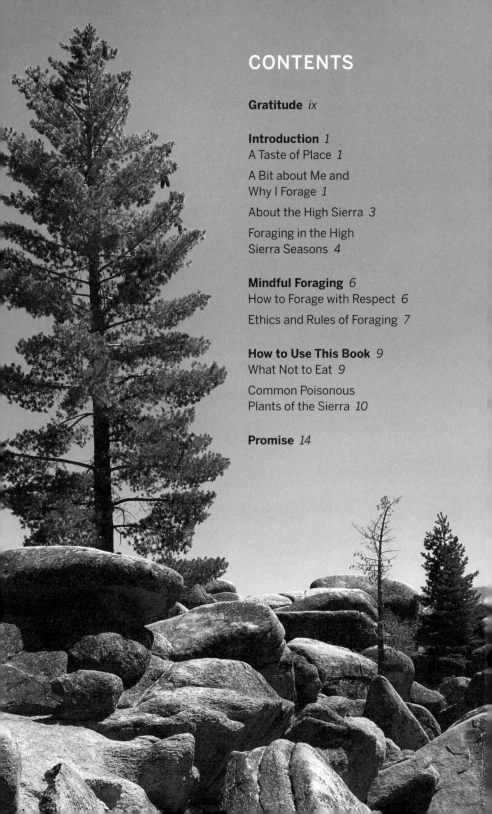

CONTENTS

EDIBLE PLANTS

Next Steps

GRATITUDE

I am deeply grateful to the plants that feed me and teach me each day I walk on this earth. I feel that they guide me in this process, and I hope I have done them justice and shared what they wished for me to share.

I am amazed by the Sierra Nevada and the deep-blue Lake Tahoe and feel incredibly blessed to call this wondrous spot my home.

I want to honor that these lands are the lands of the Maidu, Niseman, Washoe, Northern Paiute, Owens Valley Paiute-Shoshone, Sierra Miwok, Southern Miwok, Monache, and other Indigenous tribes whose names are not known to me. I revere the cultural traditions, rich relationships, and thousands of years of embodied knowledge that the Native peoples of these lands have with the plants. I have refrained from writing about their knowledge in this book and instead focus on what I know from experience and the wisdom of my teachers. With that said, I am sure much of the information about the edibility of these plants does come from local Native Americans, and I am deeply grateful for their wisdom. I recognize that my knowledge is at the preschool level compared with the wisdom held by the people of this land and welcome any feedback.

Thank you to all the conservationists past and present who have preserved much of these lands as forest and parks. I shudder to think of what would have happened without their great effort.

I am grateful to my teachers who helped me develop my love of plants: my grandmother, Eva Andler; my permaculture teacher, Penny Livingston Stark; my nature awareness teacher, Jon Young; fellow adventurer Jeff Jenkins; fellow forager Matt Berry; and coauthor of my previous book, Kevin Feinstein.

Thank you to my family and especially my children, who have foregone some game-playing and snowball-throwing hours in the interest of Mama writing her book.

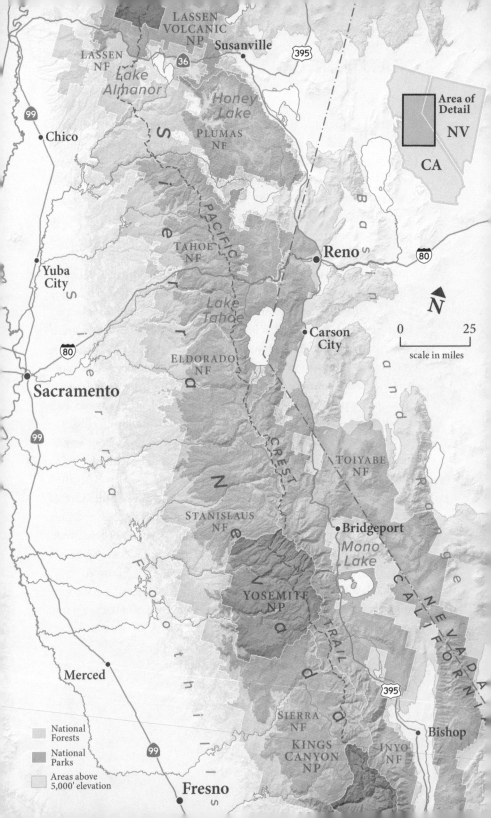

INTRODUCTION

A Taste of Place

What if you could taste a place?

What would the High Sierra taste like? Could you taste the unique flavor of one of the most beautiful, majestic spots in the world? A bit of gray spotted granite with a side of snowmelt, dipped in turquoise mountain lake, an air of Jeffrey pine, and a sprinkling of ancient volcanic rock?

I lament the loss of a truly local cuisine. I actually think about it quite often, especially while traveling. Much like many of our local accents and dialects, truly local food has disappeared into the mundane luxury of our hodgepodge of global cuisine today. Had we lived five hundred years ago, even traveling from county to county would have been a culinary adventure. For the most part, people ate what grew where they lived. Food didn't travel many miles, and the ingredients that did were unusual and highly valued. There would have been a big difference between what food tasted like or consisted of in the High Sierra as opposed to the San Francisco Bay Area, for example.

So what did the food of the High Sierra taste like? The best way to answer that now is to eat from the land—harvest the wild edibles. The wild plants grow from that very same spotted granite rock, snowmelt, turquoise water next to the Jeffrey pine, and volcanic rock. Those elements are in their plant bodies, and when we consume them they become part of us. I can taste the difference between a Bay Area nettle and a Sierra nettle, and I hope you will too.

A Bit about Me and Why I Forage

I grew up in Finland, where we have more forest than people. There is a lot of space, and many people still spend a significant part of their time off at their little cabin in the woods or by a lake. I grew up spending a lot of my time playing in nature.

Foraging was much more common in Finland than it is here. Stinging nettle soup was a common dish even in school. In the summer, the forest floor was covered in bilberries, raspberries, lingonberries, and cloudberries. In the fall, delicious chanterelle mushrooms were easy to find. We would go out as a family to pick these foods and bring them home to cook.

My grandmother also taught me about less common edibles. She would call oxalis "fox's bread" and tell me how horsetail used to be a tree in the age of the dinosaurs. She grew up in a time when knowledge about edibility and medicinal uses of plants was more common. Surprisingly, as she got older and I wrote my first book, *The Bay Area Forager*, she thought it was kind of odd that I wanted to collect nettles and wild foods. She felt that we now have so many better choices, so why should we have to eat these foods that were a necessity in wartime?

I came to the US when I was fifteen. After college when I lived in Tahoe City, I became very interested in outdoor education and started noticing many plants that looked familiar to me. I found it strange that almost no one I knew was eating wild plants back then. I started asking everyone who knew about plants about edibility; I figured there must be some edible plants here, too. I attended a permaculture and nature awareness program with Penny Livingston Stark, Jon Young, and Matt Berry, who taught me about the plants of my adopted home. Through a lot of research, experimentation, and asking around, I slowly acquired quite a bit of knowledge about edible plants in California, and even started teaching classes myself. When Kevin Feinstein and I wrote *The Bay Area Forager*, we both felt as though we were offering up information in a quick minute that had taken us years to learn—which was, of course, the right thing to do. When I first started my foraging journey, there were few good books on the subject—Euell Gibbons's work of course being an exception. Now there are now many good books and websites on foraging available for eager students of wild plants.

Even though my first foraging book was about the Bay Area, my journey with foraging California plants actually started in the High Sierra about twenty years ago. I did so much exploring and hiking while living in Tahoe City that it made sense to look for edible plants at the same time. Through hiking friends who were into lightweight camping and nature connection, I also learned that I could eat manzanita berries and nibble on fir trees. It was easy to be interested in wild edibles in the Sierra. I left the Sierra to get more education, but I brought the inspiration for wild edibles with me to the Bay Area. I continued to return to the Sierra frequently, and returned permanently a few years ago.

I love fresh, local food from the land and am ultra-cautious about what I eat. That is my basis for knowing a lot about foraging. With that said, there is still so much more to know. Some people actually subsist solely on foraged food for long periods of time. I have never done that. Please feel free to write to me with anything I've missed. I believe that the only way to restore the great wealth of information on wild plants that has been partially lost is to do it collectively.

About the High Sierra

Saying that the Sierra Nevada is an awe-inspiring mountain range is an understatement. This large mountain range referred to by John Muir as "the Range of Light" encompasses such wonders as Yosemite, Lake Tahoe, and Mount Whitney. I recently drove from Lake Tahoe to Los Angeles (most of the Sierra Nevada range) taking the mountain route, and despite the fact that I have made that trip many times, I found myself saying, "Wow, it's absolutely gorgeous here—I'm so lucky" every twenty minutes. There is so much to learn about the geology, history, and ecology of the Sierra Nevada that I highly recommend picking up one of the many books on those subjects. I also highly recommend reading John Muir or one of the many other authors who have written poetically about this place. Because this book is about wild edible plants, I will stay focused on my ground-level view rather than looking at the bigger picture, and only say a teeny bit about the majestic Sierra Nevada here.

There is great diversity of elevation, ecosystems, and plants in the Sierra Nevada. The Sierra Nevada is the longest continuous mountain range in the United States, running four hundred miles north–south and approximately seventy miles east–west. It thus covers a very large region, from Lake Almanor on the Feather River in the north, to a bit south of Bakersfield in the south. The range varies greatly in elevation as well, with lower western slopes and river valleys and dramatic eastern peaks. The highest peak is Mt. Whitney at 14,495 feet. As Edna and Ray Vizgirdas write in their book *Wild Plants of the Sierra Nevada*, "With so much topographic relief, the Sierra Nevada possesses a high diversity of plant species, and many species are endemic (restricted) to the range." Because of the topographic diversity, even though this range accounts for only 20 percent of California's land, more than half of California's flora is found here. There are ecosystems from moist and temperate to desert, including foothills, montane forests, and alpine environments.

Because of this enormous diversity, I chose to focus only on the northern areas of the range at high elevations, which I know best. I currently live in Lake Tahoe, California, and have a personal living knowledge of the plants of the region. This book is therefore most applicable to the elevations above five thousand feet in the area shown on the map, from Plumas County to the high-desert town of Bishop. It includes the high-elevation areas around Yosemite National Park. This does not mean that this book can't be very useful further south, at lower elevations, or even in mountain ranges of a different state. Many of the plants I feature in this book, especially the ones recently introduced, also grow in other environments. I just prefer to write about what I know and to be honest with you about my regional bias. Many earth-based cultures refer to their home region as the belly button of the world, and I find there to be a truth to that, which I wish more people would recognize: we are formed by our landscape. Currently, my belly button is Lake Tahoe. I hope when you pick up this book that focuses on the High Sierra, you will find it directly useful for identifying plants you will see on hikes and day-to-day. With this book at hand, you will find out more about the plants that are common, relevant, and sustainable to forage in the northern High Sierra.

Foraging in the High Sierra Seasons

One of the first questions I'm asked when I say I'm writing an edible plant guide to the High Sierra is "But is there really much to eat there? What about in the winter?" Yes, there are many wild edibles here, and yes, it's true, winter is not a great time to forage: there are very few plants to choose from during the snowy winter. It would be very hard to survive off the land in the High Sierra in winter. However, being from a cold and snowy country myself, I know that one of the blessings of the freezing winter is the abundant water and sweet berries it brings in the summer.

Here is a quick guide to what to look for in each season:

Spring: This is the season for fresh young greens and spring flowers, such as fireweed shoots, young thistles, and little yarrow.

Early summer: Now is a time of abundance. Look for blossoms of elderberries and rose, greens such as nettle and salsify, and roots and corms.

Later summer: Look for berries such as thimbleberry, gooseberry, and currant, and for mature greens such as dandelion and dock.

Fall: Nuts, seeds, and manzanita are plentiful in this season.

Winter: Look for tree bark, pine and fir needles, the occasional greens in melted or warmer areas, or leftover seeds of tall plants such as dock.

Appendix A at the back of the book is a chart of what you can expect to find in each season.

MINDFUL FORAGING

How to Forage with Respect

I invite you to sample this amazing Sierra taste that I'm talking about, but also to pause and consider the impact of your choices when you set out to enjoy the plants of the Sierra, especially if you are a visitor. So many people come to enjoy the splendors of Tahoe and the Sierra that if every one of them picked just one rare edible flower, it could exacerbate the challenges already faced by our remaining native flora in the face of development and climate change. This is something to be aware of especially in the Yosemite region, which already has an overabundance of traffic. I just ask that you stop for a minute right now and promise me that you will learn from this book to harvest with utmost care only for your own purposes, because our wild plants are a shared resource that we all must tend to and protect. If you do want to start a plant-focused foraging business, please harvest invasives only, or plant a wild garden!

When you are foraging on wild lands, watch your step just as you would if you were in your garden. I was once part of a film shoot for a travel channel where I was talking about juicy miner's lettuce. While I pointed out the plant, another forager stepped on several patches, effectively killing the plants. Don't do that, please. This is our big garden—you wouldn't step on the tomatoes you grew with great care, would you?

I have included a sustainability section in each plant description to indicate when a plant is abundant and can be readily foraged in most places, or when it is more sensitive and should only be sampled, not collected in bulk. I have intentionally left out some rare wild edibles, because part of being a respectful forager is knowing where we can do harm and holding back. Even an abundant plant population can be overharvested. So unless you're harvesting invasives and you are being part of the solution of restoring our wild meadows and forests, please only take what you need or a small sample. When you do harvest invasive plants, such as salsify, dandelion, and mullein, please be careful not to spread their seed. (Most plants are best eaten before seeding anyway.)

With all this said, I believe that knowing about the uses and edibility of our local plants is extremely important. That is why I've written this book. We have already lost too much of the deep knowledge all our ancestors carried. We can only restore it collectively. I believe that knowledge and connecting with the plants through eating them will be an essential part of restoring and protecting our local landscapes. I also hope to see us integrate a lot more local foods into our diet again—for our own good and the good of the environment. Food plants adapted to local conditions often require far fewer inputs and energy and cause far less environmental damage than introduced species. If we find that a plant we want to eat is dwindling in numbers, I hope that discovery will serve as our call to action to restore it to abundance.

We humans have a great capacity for taking care of this earth. Foraging can connect us to place and inspire that caretaking. My hope is that you will proceed with that attitude. "Leave it better than you found it" is my motto. Pick up some trash, pour some water on a patch of plants you harvested from, and remember to say thank you.

Ethics and Rules of Foraging

The following are some general foraging rules I like to go by for any location:

- Don't harvest a plant that is the only one or one of only a few of its kind in that spot.
- An often-repeated foraging rule is never to harvest more than one-third of the entire quantity. In my opinion, however, one-third is far too much; I would suggest more like one-seventh.
- Watch how the animals engage with the plants. Don't harvest something that wildlife clearly prefer.
- Consider the current condition and health of the plants. Don't harvest struggling plants at drought time or in the winter.

Most public lands have rules with regard to foraging. Please make sure you look into those before foraging on public land. Here are a few specific regulations relevant to the Sierra:

In the California State Parks, harvesting of wild foods is severely restricted: "No person shall willfully or negligently pick, dig up, cut ... any tree or plant or portion thereof, including but not limited to ... flowers, foliage, berries, fruit, grass . . . shrubs, cones, and dead wood, except in specific units when authorization by the District Superintendent or Deputy Director of Off-Highway Motor Vehicles to take berries, or gather mushrooms, or gather pine cones, or collect driftwood is posted at the headquarters of the unit to which the authorization applies." Some exceptions may exist, so check the rules before you go.

In national forests, which are federal lands run by the US Forest Service, in general harvesting "incidental amounts"—often defined as one gallon—of mushrooms and berries for personal use is allowed without a permit. Check the rules for your specific national forest. Harvesting from wilderness areas is prohibited.

With regard to Yosemite National Park, the following fruits may be gathered by hand for personal consumption, up to one pint per person per day for immediate consumption: blackberries, raspberries, elderberries, strawberries, thimbleberries, and huckleberries. Himalayan blackberries can be gathered in unlimited quantity. You can read the rules in more detail at Yosemite's website.

Bureau of Land Management (BLM) land and national wildlife refuges may be more permissive.

If you intend to forage on private land, it is prudent to ask the permission of the owner.

HOW TO USE THIS BOOK

When you are first starting out as a forager, encountering the wall of green plants and trying to start distinguishing one from another can be overwhelming. I suggest perusing this book at home first, then going out to see whether anything looks familiar and comparing what you find with the descriptions in the book. You could also use a wildflower field guide or an identifying app such as iSeek to identify plants and then look in the book to determine whether they are edible.

My intention is for this book to introduce you to eating common wild edibles of the High Sierra region and to be a useful guide to these plants. It is appropriate both for beginners and for more experienced foragers, and it is small enough that you can take it with you on a hike.

This book is not intended to be a comprehensive guide to all edible wild plants in the Sierra, and I have left out mushrooms because this is not the best region for mushroom foraging. Further, mushrooms are fungi, which is an entirely different form of life. This book is not an ethnobotanical history of the plants of the region. As I mentioned earlier, I have learned from historical accounts, but this book is based on my own experience and that of my teachers.

I love cooking and have included recipes as ideas, and I have referred to medicinal uses of plants in some places. If you are excited to learn more about these aspects of wild plants, I encourage you to check out the books by expert chefs and herbalists on these topics.

What Not to Eat

"What *shouldn't* I eat?" This is a great question—one that everyone should be asking before eating anything in the wild. The simple answer is, do not eat anything that you aren't 150 percent sure is edible.

So how do you know whether a plant is edible? The best way to learn is from someone who eats it regularly with no adverse effects. With that said, everyone's body is different, so something that works for someone else may not work for you. It is always advisable to try just a small piece of a new edible first and wait a few hours before trying more.

There are no blanket rules for knowing what is poisonous. Sayings such as "All red berries are poisonous," "Watch the animals," and the like probably originated in a particular region where they might have applied, but they are not safe assumptions. If you must eat something that you're not sure of, you can follow this process:

1. Pick a small piece of the plant. Rub it in your fingers and smell it. Wait several hours or even a day for adverse skin reactions.
2. Put a small bit of the plant on your tongue, then spit it out. Wait a day to see whether any adverse reactions develop.
3. Eat a very small piece. Wait a day to see whether any adverse reactions develop.
4. Eat a bit more. Wait a day to see whether any adverse reactions develop.

If all that goes well, you can probably eat it. Consider too that it's often best to cook unknown plants.

For you to develop the confidence to eat wild plants, I recommend that you get to know a certain place well rather than try to learn everything all at once. It's better to start in your backyard or a place you explore often and become familiar with that area and the plants there through the seasons.

Common Poisonous Plants of the Sierra

Here are a few highly toxic plants that you want to be able to recognize and know never to eat.

Poison hemlock: This plant is in the carrot family and can be easily mistaken for many edible plants, such as yampah. When it's young, it looks like a small carrot top. When older, it has a long, tall hollow stalk with umbels of small white flowers. It is very common, growing in meadows, along edges of roads, among edible greens, and even in your garden. This is the plant used in the poison that Socrates was forced to drink. Even a small piece can cause death through muscle paralysis and respiratory failure. Because there are so many look-alikes in the carrot family, it is wise for beginner foragers to avoid all of these plants.

Erratum, *The Sierra Forager*

Due to a production error, the photo on page 11 is misidentified as poison hemlock (*Conium maculatum*). For help correctly identifying poison hemlock, please consult the Jepson eFlora: https://ucjeps.berkeley.edu/eflora/

Poison hemlock

Water hemlock

Death camas lily

Red bane berry

Corn lily

Pacific yew

Water hemlock: This plant is also in the carrot family and can be easily mistaken for many edible plants, such as yampah or watercress. Water hemlock usually grows in or near water. When it is small, it looks a bit like parsley and can be hard to identify. When it is older, it's three to seven feet tall, with leaves that remind me a bit of elderberry leaves, ovate with toothed edges. The flowers of water hemlock are white and tiny and grow in umbels. It is probably most dangerous when young and easily picked along with other greens growing in or near the water, so be cautious when harvesting water greens. Again, if you're a beginner, avoid picking all members of the carrot family until you know your plants and place well.

Death camas lily: Death camas lilies are particularly dangerous because they look similar to edible camas, wild onions, and other edible plants of the lily family. They can be recognized by their white flowers, so if you are not sure whether a plant could be a death camas, it's best to wait until it flowers.

Skunk cabbage: These showy-looking plants may be called corn, but they are quite poisonous.

Red bane berry: This plant is not very common in the Sierra, but sometimes people assume that all nice-looking berries are edible. These are not.

Pacific yew: All yews are toxic. They look a bit like a fir or pine, which is why it is good to be familiar with them. Their needles are not fragrant, however, and, fortunately, yew is not very common.

The plants I've described here are a reminder to be aware while foraging. They teach us to slow down, pay attention, and harvest with respect, and not just grab handfuls of plants we think we know.

Promise

Dear reader, please promise me three things:

1. That you will not eat anything unless you are 100 percent sure it is edible
2. That you will not eat more than a "taste bite" of any plant that is more rare or a precious wildflower
3. That you will harvest and tread with respect for the plants

With that said, have fun foraging!

EDIBLE PLANTS

AMERICAN BROOKLIME/ AMERICAN SPEEDWELL

Veronica americana
Plantaginaceae (Other common edible species in this family—plantains)
Originates in temperate and arctic Asia and North America

———

Many plants that are edible strike me as such easily. Brooklime surprised me: it's quite common, but I have passed it by for many years. Somehow its beautiful blue or violet flowers and shiny-looking leaves that often turn reddish just didn't strike me as edible at first. Brooklime is in fact edible and medicinal, though quite bitter. The name "speedwell" comes from the plant's propensity to lose its petals in a short amount of time. This is not a plant that I often harvest, but it is common and good to be familiar with. I see it often near High Sierra creeks and wet meadows.

Identification: This is an annual or perennial low-growing plant, one to three feet high with opposite branching leaves. The leaves are sawtoothed and shiny, and sometimes turn red. The stem is often red. The lovely blue or purple flowers have delicate stalks and are about a quarter-inch across. This plant might remind you of a mint, but it has larger leaves.

Where to Find: Look for brooklime in very wet places near creeks, along stream edges, in wet meadows, at lake edges, and often in water.

When to Harvest: Harvest in spring before it flowers, though I've seen it even in winter.

How to Harvest: Simply pinch off a few leaves.

Poisonous Look-Alikes: Many plants look a bit like American brooklime, so you may want to wait until you see it flower for positive identification. However, it is the only common plant that looks like this (that I know of) growing directly in the water in the Sierra. There are several other less common species of speedwell. I have not been able to find good information on the edibility of these other species.

Caution: Make sure that the water source you harvest the plant from is clean, as it absorbs any toxins in the water.

Edible and Useful Parts

Leaves: You can use the leaves as a salad green or potherb similar to watercress. They are tastiest before flowering. If you need to use them after flowering, cook them like spinach. They are quite bitter and best combined with other greens. They can be made into a green tea.

Benefits: Brooklime is rich in vitamin C and flavonoids.

Sustainability: This is a native plant, so harvest only in small amounts as a trail food.

Grazing versus Harvesting

There are many foragers who are also cooks or homesteaders and focus on harvesting large amounts of food to sell or cook. My foraging style is more one of grazing like a deer. I notice an edible plant on a walk and sample it. I usually just take a small piece, a bit here and there, like a deer nibbling. It's very rare that I go out and harvest instead. I do have some annual harvests: a big nettle harvest in my backyard once a year in early summer, a chanterelle harvest in the winter on the coast, and an acorn harvest in Reno or the foothills in the fall. Other than that, I usually graze. If I'm grazing and also paying attention to my steps and surroundings, I actually feel like a deer. I feel that I'm participating in the landscape in a harmonious way, not making a big impact. The two styles can be appropriate in different contexts, and the grazing style can work for more sensitive places where foraging would not otherwise be in balance.

BIRCHES

Betula occidentalis and *Betula pendula*
Betulaceae (Other common edible species in this family—alder, hazel)
Originate in northern temperate climates worldwide

——

Birch trees are a superhero of the useful plant world. They have many gifts, from sweet replenishing sap to bark that can be made into anything from containers to shoes. With that said, the birch trees in the High Sierra are usually introduced species and not very commonly found. There are many species of birch, and their uses vary. In Finland, where I am from, birch trees are used commonly and traditionally as a cure-all and for a myriad of practical and edible purposes. Birch sap in Finland is used as a strength-giving drink similar to coconut water, and I highly recommend it, should you be able to sample some. The birches here in the California mountains are mostly planted, and I would not feel right tapping them to get sap in this dry climate, in case it should harm the tree. Harvesting young leaves is the best use of birch trees here in the High Sierra. Alders are native to the Sierra and are the more common member of the birch family found here, but they are a bit more bitter tasting than birches. The catkins of both trees are edible in the spring, but the alder catkins still have that bitterness. Alders do make a nice wilderness toothbrush, however. Simply take a little twig, cut it criss-cross on one end with a knife, and work it against a clean surface until it's soft enough to brush with.

Identification: Birch is an easy-to-identify midsize tree with beautiful white bark that's black striped. The bark is often papery and can flake off easily. The leaves are oval with serrated edges. Aspens look a lot like birch trees and are much more common. They are also edible, though not really tasty in my experience, which is why I haven't included them in this book. Birch differ from aspen in that their bark, almost a pure white, is usually much lighter than aspen bark; it is also more papery and has small horizontal lines in it. Birch leaves are serrated and sharper at the tip than aspen leaves.

Where to Find: You will usually find birches in landscaping, possibly in wet meadows.

When to Harvest: Harvest birches in spring.

How to Harvest: Remove young leaves gently.

Poisonous Look-Alikes: There are no poisonous look-alikes known.

Edible and Useful Parts

Leaves: Young leaves can be eaten cooked like a green or raw.

Catkins: The catkins are protein rich and can be eaten in the early spring.

Inner bark: The inner bark of the tree is a nutrient-dense survival food; however, the inner bark should be eaten only when the tree has to be cut down, as removing it will kill the tree.

Sap: Birch trees can be tapped in the early spring much like maples to let out a sweet-tasting sap. It can be enjoyed hot or cold.

Other uses: Birch wood is commonly used for many purposes. The bark and wood are both great for fire making. The bark can be made into containers, decorations, and clothing.

Benefits: Birches are used medicinally for a variety of conditions. It is a plant high in minerals such as potassium and calcium.

Sustainability: There is usually no concern about removing some leaves or catkins of birch trees. Tapping the sap and more invasive practices need to be carefully considered, but can be done in a sustainable way in the right setting.

Birch Leaf and Rhubarb Soda

This is a refreshing summer recipe from Finland. Rhubarb is common there, and if it is hard to find here, you can leave it out and just increase the amount of birch leaves or replace the rhubarb with some dock stalks or lamb's quarters leaves, which are in the same family. You can also try this recipe with currant or blackberry leaves.

Ingredients
- 5 cups young birch leaf
- 5 rhubarb stalks or young dock stalks, cut into pieces
- 1 lime
- 10 cups boiling water
- 1½ teaspoons citric acid
- 2 cups sugar

In a big jar, cover birch leaves and rhubarb with citric acid and water. Cover the jar and let stand overnight at room temperature. Strain the liquid and heat it up with the sugar until the sugar dissolves. Pour into bottles and store in the refrigerator. Mix the juice with bubbly water for a refreshing soda.

Birch Brooms—
A New Healthy Sauna Tradition for the Sierra?

In Finland, birches are so revered that they are considered to be very healing and even magical. One fun tradition that I have not seen here yet is the practice of using birch brooms in saunas. Finnish people make a small birch broom or bunch called *vihta* and actually hit themselves and each other with them in the sauna. This might sound a bit strange, but it's actually a very nice massage that's great for circulation and your skin. You don't hit hard, of course.

To make your own vihta, gather a small bunch of birch branches about forearm length. (I believe this could also be done with young aspen or even willow branches.) You'll want to use young branches. You then soak the bunch in a bucket of clean water overnight and take this bucket with you into the sauna. Take turns using this broom to gently hit or massage yourself from top to toe. The smell of birch leaves is very nice.

I highly recommend this healthy tradition should you own or have access to a sauna. It would be great after a day of hiking or skiing. I'm not sure that the management of a public sauna would appreciate your doing this, however. Should you want to find out more about this interesting tradition, look up "vihta."

BLACKBERRIES AND RASPBERRIES

Rubus armeniacus and other *Rubus* species
Rosaceae (Other common edible species in this family—roses, apples,
  strawberries)
Originate in Armenia and western Asia; some are native to California

It is the lucky High Sierra forager who comes across a patch of black or red raspberries. They are not common, in my experience. Blackberries are so prolific in California that although they are more unusual in the higher elevations of the Sierra, it feels strange not to mention them. Blackberries are highly invasive, and the plants are difficult to remove once they take, but their fruit is delicious. Blackberries and raspberries are foraged even by those who never forage. Who can resist a freshly baked blackberry pie? The plump berries are an easy introduction to wild foods for any tourist. The Himalayan blackberry (*Rubus armeniacus*) is the most common species. There are some native blackberries that are usually considerably smaller. I have not seen any native blackberries in the Sierra where I have gone.

Identification: Blackberries are large, usually thorny shrubs with vining thorny stems up to twelve feet high. Leaves are palmately compound, with three to five leaves per leaflet. The leaves are dark green, sometimes turning reddish, with distinct veins. The pinkish or white five-petaled flowers are about an inch across. Raspberries are similar but smaller, with red or sometimes black berries.

Where to Find: You can find these plants near human habitation, in disturbed places—just about anywhere. As I mentioned, they do not usually grow in the higher elevations of the Sierra.

When to Harvest: Harvest these plants in summer.

How to Harvest: Pinch off young leaves, flowers, and berries.

Poisonous Look-Alikes: There are none that I know of. It is good to be aware that Himalayan blackberries are sometimes sprayed with Round-Up to eradicate them. If collecting in parks, you can call the park to find out whether they spray. On a side note: if they do, I would highly suggest advocating for stopping this outdated and environmentally harmful practice.

Edible and Useful Parts

Leaves: Many people don't even realize that blackberry and raspberry leaves are nutritious, flavorful, and medicinal. The young leaves make a great flavoring, and I like to add them to pesto or just nibble on them in the spring. If you pick them young enough, they don't have thorns. Blackberry- or raspberry-leaf tea has a soft, earthy flavor and is beneficial for tonifying female systems.

Flowers: The beautiful blossoms make a nice decoration for salads and cakes and a flavorful tea as well.

Berries: Yes, the berries are delicious. Be patient and wait until they are fully ripe. Use them in pies, juices, jams, ice cream—you name it.

Benefits: Blackberries and raspberries are very high in antioxidants. They are also high in anthocyanins, which give the berries their dark color and protect the brain from oxidative stress.

Sustainability: Blackberries are very invasive. Pick all you want. Raspberries are more scarce, so use discernment.

Campfire Blackberry Pie in an Apple

I'm a big fan of cooking right on the fire and *not* a big fan of aluminum foil. If you don't mind foil, you can wrap the apples in it for a lot less of a mess, but it's kind of fun to have it be a bit messy too.

This recipe is extremely flexible. Experiment with the ingredients you have on hand. You can use whatever flour (or oats), oil, or sweetener you have. Or make a flourless version with just blackberry and apple. The kids will love it.

Ingredients
- 4 apples
- A few handfuls of blackberries
- About half a cup of whatever sweetener is easiest—sugar, maple syrup (or just leave it out)
- A bit of butter or oil
- About 1½ cups flour of any kind

Make a dough by mixing a bit of oil or butter with the flour and just enough water to make it mixable. Add the blackberries and sugar. Core out the apples, leaving the bottom intact. Fill the core with the dough, but not all the way to the top. Place in coals or on a barbecue grate, or wrap in foil. Cook until the blackberries bubble and the apple is soft. Let it cool down; it will be really hot. You can also use the intact peel of an orange instead of an apple to hold the pie dough.

BRODIAEA AND BLUE DICKS

Brodiaea spp., *Dichelostemma* spp., and *Dipterostemon capitatus*
Asparagaceae (Other common edible species in this family—asparagus,
   agave, yucca)
Originate on the west coasts of North and South America

——

Brodiaea, wild hyacinth, cluster lily, fool's onion, blue dicks, ookow, grass nut, pretty face—there sure are many names for these well-loved plants. It's no wonder, either, as this tasty and unusually nutritious plant would have been a welcome sight to anyone living in the wilderness. There are many species of *Brodiaea* in the Sierra. The ones found at the higher altitudes are harvest brodiaea (*Brodiaea elegans*), manyflowered brodiaea (*Dichelostemma multiflorum*), Bridge's brodiaea (*Triteleia bridgesii*), pretty face (*Triteleia ixiodes*), and hyacinth brodiaea (*Triteleia hyacinthina*), which is pictured here. I commonly see the white wild hyacinths where I live in Tahoe, the others not so much. All of them are members of the Brodiaeoideae subfamily and are much alike. Digging up their small corms may feel very laborious, but if you learn how to harvest them properly so that you help the plant flourish, they are well worth the effort.

Identification: These low-growing perennial plants grow from corms. Species vary in height from one to thirty-six inches tall. The leaves are grass-like and the stem very straight. The leaves are basal, meaning that they grow from the bottom of the plant. The small but showy flowers grow in clusters of one to ten and are purple, blue, or white. There is one species with light-yellow flowers, named "pretty face."

Where to Find: You can find these plants in moist soil, heavy clay soils, rocky areas, and open areas.

When to Harvest: Harvest in spring and summer.

How to Harvest: How you harvest these precious native plants is very important: done correctly, you enhance their growth; done incorrectly, you lessen their numbers.

The corms of *Brodiaea* actually need dividing every three to five years so that they can disperse and increase in numbers. This makes it the perfect plant to forage for those who know what they're doing. To sustainably harvest *Brodiaea* corms, first make sure you have the right tools so as not to pull the plant out without its corm, which is very easy to do. It is often difficult to dig out the corms because of the heavy soils they grow in, so bring a hori hori (Japanese gardening knife), trowel, small shovel, or sharpened fire-hardened stick. Dig deep into the soil under the plant so as not to harm the corm or roots. Many plants have several corms, in which case taking one corm to eat and separating the others and replanting them a few inches apart from one another will spread the plant and actually enhance its growth by loosening the soil around it. If the plant has only one corm, you can just leave it or cut it in half to propagate it that way. Cutting it in half is not as successful a propagation method, however, as doing so sometimes leaves the corm more vulnerable, so separating the corms is best whenever possible.

Poisonous Look-Alikes: Lilies and death camas can be mistaken for brodiaea and blue dicks. Death camas flowers are abundant and grow off the stem, not in an umbel as do *Brodiaea* flowers. Because there are many toxic members of the lily family, it is good to delay harvesting until the plants flower. Members of the *Brodiaea* genus often flower earlier than camas lilies.

Edible and Useful Parts

Flowers: You can add the flowers to salads or eat them raw.

Corms: The corms of these plants are delicious and taste a bit like a blend of an onion and a potato. They can be eaten raw, cooked, or dried and ground into flour. Just remove the outer skin and prepare as you choose. Some of them have a slightly mucilaginous (slimy) texture, so they tend to be tastier cooked. Simply steam them or boil them with a bit of salt, much as you would cook potatoes. The flour can be used for baking bread or pancakes.

Benefits: From a survival and trail-food perspective, these are one of the few wild edible plants in the region that are starchy and therefore make you feel more full than you would just eating greens.

Sustainability: These are beautiful wildflowers native to our region. Harvest only in areas where they are clearly abundant unless you are skilled at doing a restoration project with them. If you harvest them correctly, there can be a synergy between the forager and the plant. Brodiaeas are great plants to cultivate in your own garden. However, because many of us do not have access to private land where we can plant brodiaeas, please harvest only one to sample unless you are able to propagate them as described earlier and to build a long-term relationship with this plant.

Corms, Tubers, Roots, and Bulbs— What's the Difference?

If you thought plants weren't smart, think again. I'm often amazed by the diversity of survival techniques that plants have developed. One very successful adaptation that many species have evolved to use is a form of underground storage for saving nutrients and genetic information so that even if the mother plant dies due to difficult conditions, the plant is able to regrow at a more suitable time, drawing from its "warehouse" belowground.

Many underground parts of plants are very tasty and nutritious. At first glance, we might be tempted to call all of them roots. Many of us are familiar with bulbs from planting tulips in the garden, but what are corms and tubers? Here is a quick guide:

Root. The underground part of a plant that absorbs water and nutrients and holds the plant in place. Often thin with hairlike extensions. Examples of common edible roots include carrot, beet, and salsify.

Bulb. An underground stem or the dormant stage of a plant where it stores its energy. In a way, you can think of it as next year's plant waiting to grow. Bulbs are covered with a protective layer called a tunic. Examples of common edible bulbs are onion and garlic.

Corm. A fleshy underground stem that some plants use in order to store energy in adverse conditions (e.g., cold, heat, or drought). Corms, like bulbs, are covered by a protective layer called a tunic. Unlike bulbs, they don't grow in layers. Think sweet potato versus onion. Corms can be dug up and saved and then replanted next season if desired. Examples of common edible corms are sweet potato and celeriac.

Tuber. A swollen stem that stores energy for later use. It does not have a tunic layer as corms and bulbs do. Examples of common edible tubers include potato and ginger.

So now you can be educational and ask, "How do your mashed tubers taste?" at the dinner table.

BUSH CHINQUAPIN

Chrysolepis sempervirens
Fagaceae (Other common edible species in this family—oaks, beeches)
Originates in the western United States

———

Chinquapin seeds must be delicious, because they are protected by a fortress of spines, making them look like little hedgehogs on a bush. They are a favorite of many animals, so unless you find the seeds at just the right time, you may not have a chance to sample one, or you may find the nuts inside the shells to be rotted or even empty. If you do get lucky and find some, they are sweet and tasty. There are actually two species of chinquapin on the West Coast: one a tree, the other a shrub. There are some tree-variety chinquapins in the northern Sierra Nevada, but you are more likely to encounter the bush version, the bush chinquapin.

Identification: Bush chinquapin is an evergreen shrub that grows to a height of seven feet, with hardy oblong leaves that are green on top and golden yellow on the bottom. The flowers are small. The fruit is notable, with its very spiny protective shell. There are three edible seeds inside.

Where to Find: This plant grows on steep, often south-facing rocky and dry slopes; in open woods; and in partial shade.

When to Harvest: Harvest the nuts in summer.

How to Harvest: Bring gloves to protect yourself from the spines (unless you have really tough hands) and simply harvest the nuts off of the shrub.

Poisonous Look-Alikes: There are none to my knowledge.

Edible and Useful Parts

Nuts: The nuts inside the spiny shells are edible and delicious. Wait until the burrs are just turning brown and easy to pick, but not falling off yet. Then harvest and simply crack the spiny shell open and remove the three nuts. The nuts should be shiny. You can eat them raw or roast them. Should you happen on a large supply, they can be used like nuts in any sweet recipe or baked into bread. I find these to be so rare, however, that it's best to just sample a few and not harvest enough for a recipe.

Benefits: Like other nuts, chinquapins are high in protein.

Sustainability: These are fairly rare shrubs native to the area. Please do not harvest in quantity. Nibble on one or two only.

CATTAILS

Typha spp.
Typhaceae
Typha latifolia originates in North America, *Typha angustifolia* in Europe

___

Cattails are a generous superstar of the edible plant world. Wild-food expert and author of many foraging books, Euell Gibbons, considered the cattail "the supermarket of the swamps" because of its multiple uses. Indeed, cattails have so much to offer that entire books have been written just about them. What I have written here is an introduction, and I encourage you to look up more uses and recipes for cattails. These plants are widely available around the world. I have used cattail in various ways, ranging from hats to dolls to flour for bread to a swampy-tasting snack. Cattail tastes sweet, and some part of it is available in most seasons. It does often take on the flavor and filth of the water it's in, so it's important to harvest it where it grows in clean water. With the exception of the pollen, I do not eat it unless I know the water is clean.

Identification: Cattail is a giant grass-like perennial plant that has a big brown sausage-like flower head. It's quite unmistakable. Its leaves are long and narrow. It grows three to ten feet tall, usually in water or next to it. The native species *Typha latifolia* is very common. It and the nonnative *Typha angustifolia* are closely related and sometimes even hybridize when they grow in the same place.

Where to Find: Cattails are very common in water—ponds, marshes, and edges of lakes.

When to Harvest: The various parts can be harvested in spring, summer, and fall.

How to Harvest: Cut off the desired part of the plant. To collect pollen, put a bag over the flower and shake the pollen into the bag.

Poisonous Look-Alikes: There are no poisonous look-alikes I'm aware of. The young shoots could possibly resemble the shoot of another plant, so be more cautious with those.

Edible and Useful Parts

Green flower heads: These start forming in early summer. The sheath can be peeled off and the inside boiled or cooked and eaten like corn on the cob with a bit of salt and butter. Much like corn, the core is not edible.

Seeds: In late summer, the dry seeds can be collected and ground into flour, as can the entire female flower head.

Young shoots and stalks: When the shoots and stalks first emerge in spring, they are tender and sweet. I find the taste to be like cucumber. They can be eaten raw, boiled, or fried.

Pollen: The bright-yellow pollen is sweet and fun to collect in the early summer, usually in June. Look out for it, as it will be very prolific for a while and then be gone. In the right season, just shake the male flower parts—which are smaller and found at the top of the female sausage-like flower—into a container, or, better yet, put a bag over the flower so the wind doesn't catch it. Cattail pollen makes a protein-rich flour to add to baked goods, smoothies, cereal, or pancakes.

Rhizomes: These are the swollen underwater stems of the cattails. They are best harvested in fall or even winter. Simply follow the stem of the cattail to the root and pull off some of the rhizomes. Wash and scrub them carefully— otherwise, they will taste like mud—and take off any smaller roots, leaving only the larger rhizome. You can cook it or bake it, then eat it, simply discarding the fibrous parts with your teeth. I recommend cooking the rhizomes rather than eating them raw, as they can cause stomach upset otherwise.

Other uses: You can also make a finer starch for baking or other uses. I find it easier to use the dry method (see the next paragraph for the wet method): dry the rhizomes in the oven or a dehydrator and then pound them until the fibrous parts separate.

The resulting powder can then be sifted into a flour and used for baking biscuits, pancakes, or breads.

If you are in a hurry or don't have a good way to dehydrate foods without them rotting, you can use the wet method: place the cleaned rhizomes in a bowl of water and separate the starch from the fiber with your hands under the water. When they are separated, you can pour the water through a sieve. The starch will settle to the bottom, and you can pour off any excess water.

One part of the cattail you do not want to eat is the male flower head once it matures. It will be filled with fluff. This fluff is useful, from tinder to pillow stuffing, and the entire flower head can be dipped into oil and lit on fire as a lantern. Cattail leaves are also a great fiber and very useful for making rope and weaving.

Benefits: Cattails are very nutrient dense.

Sustainability: Cattails spread through both seed and root rhizomes, and are therefore prolific. *Typha angustifolia* is invasive in many areas, and it is helpful to harvest it.

Cattail Power Cookies

Instead of using traditional protein powder in this cookie, use cattail pollen powder.

Ingredients

- 2 cups flour (any kind you like to use for baking)
- 8 tablespoons cattail pollen (or substitute more for up to half the flour if you have collected enough)
- 1 teaspoon baking soda
- Pinch of salt
- 2 sticks butter or coconut oil
- 2 eggs
- 1 teaspoon vanilla extract
- ½ cup sweetener of your choice; I like coconut sugar or date syrup
- 1 cup nuts, wild seeds, chocolate chips, carob chips, raisins— whatever you like in your cookies!

Preheat oven to 375°. Mix the dry ingredients together. Melt the butter and mix the wet ingredients into the dry ingredients. Add the nuts or other yummies. Drop by teaspoonfuls onto a greased cookie sheet. Bake for 9–11 minutes until golden brown.

CINQUEFOILS

Potentilla spp.
Rosaceae (Other common edible species in this family—roses, apples,
   strawberries, raspberries)
Originate in the eastern Mediterranean

—

When you see a plant with what looks like strawberry leaves but then realize
it's not a strawberry after all because it has more leaves, you are probably
looking at a cinquefoil. That's what I've experienced, anyway! Cinquefoils are
very common where I live in the Tahoe area. The good news is that cinquefoils, like their relatives strawberries, are edible, just not as tasty. Cinquefoil
means "five leaved," which refers to the number of leaflets in the beautiful
compound leaves. They start popping up in the Sierra in early spring and then
keep growing and expanding with their runners until late summer. I like the
green taste of the fresh leaves. There are thirteen types of cinquefoil in the
High Sierra. Some varieties fruit more than others and are tastier than others.

Identification: Cinquefoil is a
low-growing herbaceous plant up to
two inches tall. It has palmately compound leaves, almost like the palm of
a hand, making a maple leaf sort of
shape, with five to seven leaflets with
serrated edges. They are very similar
to strawberry leaves except that there
are more leaflets. The leaves and
stems are hairy. Its flowers look like
strawberry flowers, except that they
are yellow. The fruit also looks like a
strawberry, but it is smaller, rounder,
and more seedy.

Where to Find: You can find cinquefoil near human habitation, in sunny
openings in coniferous forests, along
roads, and in the sun.

When to Harvest: Harvest in the
spring and summer.

How to Harvest: Pinch off the
desired part.

Poisonous Look-Alikes: There are
none that I can think of.

Edible and Useful Parts

Leaves and stems: These can be eaten
raw or cooked, or made into tea. The
young leaves are best in flavor.

Flowers: You can eat the flowers raw
or use them for decoration.

Fruit: It can be eaten fully ripe
or unripe.

Roots: Some other foragers say they
can be eaten, but I have not tried
them myself.

Benefits: Cinquefoils are high in vitamins C and K, folate, and potassium.

Sustainability: Cinquefoils are
very common.

Wild-Leaf Sprinkle

This is a nutrient- and mineral-rich wild-leaf sprinkle that you can use on top of pastas, in soups, or in any dish that needs a bit more wildness added to it. The recipe works with whatever edible plants you have on hand.

Ingredients
- 1 cup of an assortment of dried wild green leaves—for example, cinquefoil, nettle, dandelion, blackberry, and currant
- Salt
- Sesame seeds (optional)

Crush the fully dried leaves and push them through a metal sieve to remove any woody parts. Put them in a jar and shake with salt and sesame seeds.

CLEAVERS/BEDSTRAWS

Galium spp.
Rubiaceae (Other common edible species in this family—coffee, madder)
Originate in California, North America, Europe, and western Asia

---

Some foragers joke that you don't need to find this plant—it will find you. *Cleave* means both "to cut apart" and "to stick together"—this plant is named for its tendency to attach itself to you. It's fun to teach kids about this plant, as it can be used as a natural plant badge by sticking a piece of it onto clothing. It's not only fun and abundant but also tasty and nutritious, with many health benefits. This is one of those easy-to-identify, abundant plants that even a brand-new forager can harvest with ease. All species of cleavers are reported to be edible, so if you see a plant with square stems and whorled leaves, you are in safe territory. *Galium aparine* is the specific species of this plant that is most commonly harvested.

Identification: Cleavers are annual or perennial low-growing creeping plants with distinct whorls of leaves, like a flower of leaves around the stem. Stems are square. Some cleaver types are very rough with tiny hooked hairs, and cling to things—thus the nickname I use with kids: "Velcro plant." Cleavers can be very delicate or tangle together in large rough bunches where stems can be up to six feet in length. Flowers are tiny and white, with four petals.

Where to Find: You can find this plant just about anywhere in proximity to humans—from cracks of sidewalks to forests and open woodlands. It prefers partial shade and a bit of moisture.

When to Harvest: Harvest in spring, as early as possible, before it flowers.

How to Harvest: Simply pinch a stem.

Poisonous Look-Alikes: There are none that I know of.

Edible and Useful Parts

Leaves and stems: Try to pick these when they're young—the younger they are, the less rough their texture. Cleavers have a pleasant soft, green flavor. If their texture weren't so rough, they would be a popular edible green. Use them in salad or as a leafy green when they are young and tender. Blend them into smoothies, dressings, and pesto when they are rougher. Make them into a nourishing tea anytime.

Fruit: The fruit, which looks like little spiked green balls, can be dried and roasted to make a coffee substitute.

Other uses: Cleavers have other uses as well. The name "bedstraw" comes from its use for mattress stuffing in Europe. The name "galium" is originally from *gala,* the Greek word for milk; cleavers are reported to have been used for curdling and coagulating milk for cheese making. The roots of cleavers make a red dye.

Benefits: Cleavers are tonifying and very high in minerals. Many herbalists use them to help alleviate a wide range of diseases and symptoms.

Sustainability: *Galium aparine* is a very widespread and abundant plant, often invasive, so harvest freely.

However, please be aware that other *Galium* species may be very rare, so if the plant is not fairly long and hardy and doesn't stick to you easily, it could be a rarer species.

Cleansing Cleaver Smoothie

Cleavers appear just at the right time for a spring cleanse. Try this variation or make up your own green smoothie recipe.

Ingredients
- 1 green apple cut in pieces, seeds removed
- 4 stalks celery
- ½ lemon with skin on, well rinsed
- ½ cucumber
- Handful of young cleavers, well washed
- Handful of other wild herbs, such as nettle, chickweed, dandelion greens, yarrow, plantain, or miner's lettuce. Choose the amount based on your personal taste and needs.
- 1 small piece of ginger

Put ingredients in blender and blend on high for a few minutes. Enjoy your nourishing and cleansing drink!

CLOVERS

Trifolium spp.
Fabaceae (Other common edible species in this family—legumes, peas)
Originate in North America, Europe, western Asia, and northwest Africa

___

As common as clover is, most people don't think of eating it. It's true that clover leaves are perhaps not the tastiest green and cause bloating, so that perhaps explains why they wouldn't be a forager's first choice. Many clover *blossoms*, however, are delicious and also very beautiful. The health benefits of clovers and their ready availability make them a worthwhile plant to gather.

Identification: *Trifolium* means "three leaves." Clovers have leaves with usually three leaflets (sometimes four, if you are lucky) that are attached to each other at the center. The flowers are on a spike and are purple, pink, yellow, or white. These low-growing annual plants can be up to a foot-and-a-half tall, though most are shorter and some are creeping. There are many different species in the Sierra. The ones that occur here at higher altitudes are little hop clover (*T. dubium*), Lemmon's clover (*T. lemmonii*), long-stalked clover (*T. longipes*), whitetip clover (*T. variegatum*), and springbank clover (*T. wormskioldii*). Cultivated red and white clovers also occur near housing, especially in lawns. All species are edible as far as I know, but I have sampled only the common ones.

Where to Find: You can find clovers in moist soil, on grassy slopes, in gravel, in lawns, and near habitation.

When to Harvest: Harvest clovers in spring and summer.

How to Harvest: Carefully pinch off the flower or leaf.

Poisonous Look-Alikes: There are no poisonous look-alikes with three-leaved leaflets to my knowledge. Many people confuse sorrels with clovers, as they have similar leaves, but they are also edible.

Edible and Useful Parts

All parts of clovers are edible.

Leaves: The leaves are high in protein, as the plant is in the pea family. Unfortunately, like their bean cousins, they can cause bloating when eaten in large quantities. To avoid this problem, it can be helpful to soak them in salt water for several hours before eating. They can be eaten cooked or raw. When soaked and then dried, they can be made into a high-protein flour.

Flowers: Clover flowers make a beautiful garnish, decorative salad, and lightly honey-flavored tea. They can also be dried and ground into a flour. They are tasty raw or cooked, and I find them to be the best part of clover to eat.

Seeds: These are also edible, but they can be cumbersome to collect.

Benefits: Clovers are high in protein and minerals, and some herbalists use their flowers medicinally.

Sustainability: This varies depending on the species. Common red and white clovers are abundant, though caution is warranted due to chemicals used in lawns. The ones that grow in wilder lands are probably best let be, though sometimes you can find large fields of clover, so use your judgment. Clover is a great alternative or companion plant in a lawn, as it fixes nitrogen and therefore doesn't require fertilizer, so consider planting it at home and eating your lawn!

Clover Blossom Pudding

This is a sweet, nutritious, and beautiful pudding. I adapted this from Danielle Prohom Olson's "White Clover Snow" recipe, which she adapted from an old pioneer recipe for her website gathervictoria.com. My pudding is not always white but sometimes purple or pink. It can be made dairy free if desired. It's fun and nutritious for kids or beautiful and romantic for an adult soiree or even a valentine.

Ingredients
- 1 tablespoon gelatin (I recommend using high-quality grass-fed gelatin)
- 1½ cups lemonade
- ¼ cup of honey (clover honey if you have it)
- 1 cup plain Greek yogurt or dairy-free yogurt (best to avoid coconut so as not to mask the flavor of the blossoms)
- 2 cups clover blossoms

   Optional: If you want to change the color, use a different type of mild or watered-down juice—for example, elderberry for purple, cherry for pink.

Dissolve gelatin in ¼ cup lemonade. Puree lemonade, clover blossoms, and honey in a blender. Pour the mixture into a pot and bring to a simmer. Stir in the gelatin. Remove from heat, pour into your choice of container, and place in the fridge to gel. When the mixture has gelled, add the yogurt and stir. Put containers back in the fridge and let them sit for several hours until fully stiff. Garnish with clover blossoms.

COMMON CAMAS LILY

Camassia quamash
Asparagaceae (Other common edible species in this family—asparagus,
   agave, yucca)
Originates in North America

It is unusual that one of the most poisonous plants in the region and one of the most edible plants in the region are closely related. The white-flowered death camas lily is indeed something to watch out for, as its name implies, but its blue-flowered cousin is delicious and edible. The two are often found in the same area, so it is important to be mindful and possibly wait until the plants flower to be sure of your identification—though for better flavor, harvest after they've finished flowering. These spring and early summertime beauties will often color an entire meadow blue with their flowers. These gorgeous wildflowers are rarer these days, so we need to support and protect them. I am covering them here only because of their important food value.

Identification: This low-growing plant grows up to three feet tall from a basal rosette of straight, grass-like leaves. It has showy six-part flowers ranging from bright blue to violet, with yellow stamens. Its edible bulbs have a dark-colored outer covering.

Where to Find: You can find camas lily in sunny wet meadows, fields, and marshes.

When to Harvest: Harvest in spring and early summer.

How to Harvest: Dig out the bulb carefully with a shovel, trowel, or hardened stick.

Poisonous Look-Alikes: Beware death camas lily and possibly other poisonous lilies. Common camas is easy to identify when in flower, but often the bulbs are tastier before it flowers, which is what makes harvesting tricky. This is an excellent example of why it's important to get to know a place and its plants in all seasons before you harvest from it. Once you've identified a blue camas plant for certain when it flowers, you can gather the plant with more confidence the next spring.

Some other identification tips: Death camas is significantly larger. Blue camas lilies tend to have a lot more veins in their leaves than do death camas. Death camas leaves tend to break when you press on the slight indentation in the leaves; blue camas do not. As I said in the previous paragraph, however, your best bet is to gain more experience of the place you intend to forage before foraging anything with a significant poisonous look-alike.

Edible and Useful Parts

Bulb: The bulb is edible when cooked and has a sweet, nutty flavor. It can even be mashed or dried and made into cakes or breads, as it is very starchy.

Benefits: Common camas lily is a starchy and nutritious food.

Sustainability: A plant dies when you eat its bulb. Although blue camas lilies still cover entire meadows in many parts of the Sierra and may seem very abundant, they used to cover many more. So I recommend sampling only one, and only in very abundant areas. Otherwise, let it be, knowing that you can identify it to sustain yourself if you are ever in a survival situation. You can instead collect or purchase some blue camas seeds and plant them in the garden or the meadow on your property. Please do that.

Clover and blue camas

COW PARSNIP

Heracleum maximum
Apiaceae (Other common edible species in this family—carrots,
  dill, parsley)
Originates in North America

—

I love the Latin name of this plant, which puts "Herculean" and "maximum" together, doubly emphasizing the size of this truly large plant. Cow parsnip is a very showy plant indeed, and an interesting one. In its full-grown state, it is hard to confuse with its deadly poisonous cousins water hemlock and poison hemlock, but it is phototoxic, which means that it can cause a very bad sunburn on bare skin and has to be harvested with gloves on. The flavor of the full-grown plant can be intense, and it's therefore not always a foraging favorite. Despite this, the young shoots and greens can be quite tasty. The flavor of cow parsnip depends a lot on where it grows: it is very bitter in some areas and milder in others. Sample the plants in your area to find out.

Identification: Cow parsnip is a large-leaved plant growing up to seven feet tall or taller. The lobed leaves are almost like a giant maple leaf, and the stalks are similar to an overgrown celery. The white flowers grow in large umbels, which are clusters that look somewhat like upside-down umbrellas.

Where to Find: You can usually find cow parsnip growing in moist soils in partial shade or sun.

When to Harvest: Harvest in spring or summer.

How to Harvest: Pinch off young leaves or cut young stalks; dig up the root or underground stalks. Remember to wear gloves.

Poisonous Look-Alikes: Water hemlock and poison hemlock can be mistaken for cow parsnip, though cow parsnip leaves and stalks are much bigger, the leaves are more entire and look less like carrot leaves, and the plant does not usually grow in water.

Edible and Useful Parts

Flowers: Blossoms can be fried or cooked in spring.

Seeds: Dried seeds can be used as a spice ground or whole.

Young shoots: Growing both above- and belowground, these are probably the tastiest part of cow parsnip. You can boil, steam, or blanch them.

Young stalks: Peel and cook the young stalks, but as noted, you will want to avoid harvesting older plants.

Roots: The root can be eaten if it is cooked for a long time, but there are mixed reports of its flavor. I have not tried it myself.

Note that mature leaves and seeds can have an analgesic effect, numbing the mouth.

Benefits: Cow parsnip is high in fiber and has some medicinal uses as well.

Sustainability: This plant can be very common in some places and rare in others. Harvest with moderation unless it's very abundant.

Sautéed Wild Green Scramble

This is a simple way to start your day off with healthy wild foraged greens. You can use whatever greens are in season and supplement with other greens if necessary.

Ingredients
- About 5 cups of an assortment of wild greens, such as cow parsnip, dandelion, and sheep sorrel
- ½ onion, chopped
- Butter
- 2 eggs

Fry the onion in butter until caramelized. Add the wild greens. Crack the eggs on top and mix it all up. A yummy wild breakfast. For a vegan version, you can replace the eggs with tofu or other vegetables.

CRAB APPLES

Peraphyllum ramosissimum and *Malus* spp.
Rosaceae (Other common edible species in this family—roses, apples,
   strawberries, raspberries)
Originate in North America

——

When you see a tree with little apple-like fruit on it and wonder what it is, most of the time it's a crab apple. I often see them growing in Tahoe and Truckee parks where they were most likely planted by someone who liked crab apple jelly or admired their blossoms. Although their fruit is not as tasty as apples, it is still sweet, especially when cooked, and crab apple trees are far more disease and pest resistant. The bees also enjoy their blossoms in the spring. Other than in parks, they can also be found on dry slopes with pinyon pines and junipers. Some trees that look like wild crab apples may just be feral apple root stock that has escaped the garden, in which case they are still commonly called crab apples, but are in the genus *Malus*; those are also edible.

Identification: Wild crab apple is a small tree up to eighteen feet tall. The leaves are small and ovate, and the branches twiggy. The white flowers are usually five petaled with yellow or green centers. The fruit is up to an inch-and-a-half across, but often smaller. Crab apples are reddish green when unripe and yellowish orange to reddish when ripe. Do not harvest them too early—they won't taste good.

Where to Find: Crab apple trees grow near human habitation or on dry sunny slopes in the eastern Sierra.

When to Harvest: Harvest the fruit in fall.

How to Harvest: Be sure to pick the fruit only when fully ripe. Crab apples aren't good when green or a bit yellow.

Poisonous Look-Alikes: Crab apples could be mistaken for poisonous berries, but the fruit is much bigger. If the fruit is smaller than a quarter, do not confuse it for a crab apple.

Edible and Useful Parts

Fruit: Eat fully ripe fruit raw or cooked. It can be used in desserts, jellies, and jams. Discard the seeds.

Benefits: Crab apples tend to be a good source of vitamin C and fiber. They are reported to help protect against heart disease and cancer.

Sustainability: They are fairly rare. The ones in parks are fair game, but in the case of trees in the wild, I would harvest only a few fruits and leave the rest for wildlife.

Crab Apple Muffins

Old-fashioned muffins are a great way to use crab apples, which can be either sweet or tart. It's best to chop them small in case they are tart.

Ingredients
- 2½ cups crab apples, cored and chopped into pieces
- 2 eggs
- ¼ cup sugar or other sweetener of your choice
- ½ cup melted butter or vegan substitute
- ½ cup milk or nondairy milk
- 1 teaspoon cinnamon
- 1 teaspoon vanilla
- 1 teaspoon nutmeg
- 1 teaspoon baking powder
- 2 cups flour or gluten-free flour

Preheat oven to 350°. Mix eggs, sugar, butter, and milk in a bowl, in that order. Add cinnamon, vanilla, and nutmeg. Add baking powder and flour. Fold in the crab apples. Pour into greased muffin tins. Bake for 18–20 minutes and let cool. Serve for breakfast, perhaps with a wild-green smoothie.

DANDELION

Taraxacum officinale
Asteraceae (Other common edible species in this family—daisies, artichokes, thistles, sunflowers)
Originates in Eurasia and North America

———

Dandelion, the poster child of the wild edible weed world, may not be the most wild of the wild edibles, but it has many health benefits and is abundant in the Sierra. There are so many dandelions where I live in Tahoe and they look so delicious that it was hard to choose which photo to use. Most dandelions do taste quite bitter, so I use them sparingly, bitter not being my favorite taste. However, the Sierra dandelions are actually among the best I've tasted, growing as they do with an abundance of clean water and healthy soil, and I highly recommend them.

Identification: Dandelions are low-growing biannual herbaceous plants, growing from a basal rosette of scissor-edged leaves. The showy yellow flower grows atop a straight stem that is hollow inside. Like many Asteraceae family members, it exudes a bitter milky sap when broken. Many people know what a dandelion looks like, but some confuse it with other similar plants in the same family. There are many yellow-flowered wild lettuces and thistles, for example. None of them are poisonous, but many can be very bitter.

Where to Find: Dandelions flourish near human habitation, in moist rich soils, and on lawns.

When to Harvest: Harvest dandelions in spring and summer.

How to Harvest: Pinch off leaves, pick the flower, or dig up the root.

Poisonous Look-Alikes: There are none that I know of.

Caution: Because dandelions grow in urban areas, stay alert for pesticide use and watch out for potential contamination from dog feces.

Edible and Useful Parts

Leaves: The leaves can be eaten raw in salads or cooked as a stir-fry or in soup or an omelet.

Flowers: The flowers are maybe my favorite part of dandelions to eat. They can be eaten raw or cooked or even used for beverages such as dandelion wine.

Roots: The root can be roasted and dried and ground into a coffee substitute; it is healthier than coffee (though most people still seem to prefer coffee). My grandparents drank it during wartime in Finland when coffee was unavailable. Dandelion tea is easy to find in health food stores.

Benefits: Dandelions, like many bitter foods, are good for the liver. They are a source of vitamins A, C, and K and many minerals.

Sustainability: Dandelions are a common and abundant plant. They can also be invasive. Harvest freely, but be mindful of respectful harvesting rules covered earlier in the book.

Frivolous Dandelion Fritters

Dandelion flowers' shape makes them particularly showy to fry in dough: every crispy bite reveals a bright-yellow center. These are a fun and tasty treat served with a bit of honey or ice cream, or savory as a side dish to a wild edible soup, such as nettle soup.

Ingredients
- 2 cups dandelion blossoms still on their stalks, freshly collected so that they are not closed or wilted yet

Batter:
- 1 cup milk (dairy or nondairy)
- 1 egg
- 1 cup flour
- 1 cup corn meal
- Pinch of salt

- 2 cups high-oleic oil for frying, such as coconut oil

Whisk together the ingredients for batter. Heat the oil to medium heat. Grab a dandelion flower by the stalk, dip it in the batter, and then dip it into the oil. Fry until golden brown. Place on a surface with paper towels to drain the oil. Repeat until all flowers are fried. Let cool and serve. You can fry several at a time if you want, but that causes the oil temperature to drop, so just be careful to bring the oil temperature up between batches.

Suburban Sierra?

When we think of foraging in the Sierra, we probably imagine being in forests and on mountains on backpacking trips, eating wild plants far from civilization. Supplementing backpacking fare with some wild edibles is certainly one great foraging option in the Sierra. Another option, perhaps one that people think of less often, is to harvest the more invasive plants near the numerous High Sierra towns. Many times there are delicious wild plants right next to the restaurant you are eating in or outside your Airbnb or in your backyard. These suburban Sierra edibles can often be more sustainable to harvest in large amounts than the ones out in the mountains. The areas in the Sierra where many people have settled also are often wetter and have juicier plants than the dry slopes. I do much of my significant foraging in the less wild parts of the Sierra, though I do also enjoy grazing when on a multiday wilderness trip.

DOCK

Rumex crispus
Polygonaceae (Other common edible species in this family—buckwheat, rhubarb)
Originates in Europe and western Asia

———

Dock is a very common plant, and sometimes we don't give common things enough credit. It is very hardy, often the last plant standing in drought and snow. I like to see dock seed stalks sticking out of the snow in the late fall and early winter, and collect their easy-to-detach seeds when not much else is available. Dock seeds are encased in the remains of the flower that produced them, forming what looks like a tiny boat, enabling them to float on water and attach to debris and other plants. No wonder this plant is everywhere! Dock is very useful, too: it is edible and medicinal and can even be used as a natural dye.

Identification: Dock is a tall, leafy green plant with a basal rosette of large oblong leaves and a tall flower stem up to four feet high, with small green flowers. Leaves can have curly edges or be reddish depending on the exact species. Note the clear vein through the middle and the smaller veins that are all very visible. Seeds are noticeable in a big red cluster at the top of the plant.

Where to Find: Find dock in waste places, near human habitation, near water, in meadows, and on lawns. It is a very widely spread plant.

When to Harvest: You can harvest dock all year round.

How to Harvest: Dig up the root, remove leaves with care, or pull off some seeds.

Poisonous Look-Alikes: There are none that I know of.

Caution: One should not eat a lot of raw dock, as it is high in oxalic acid. When eating larger amounts, be sure to cook it once and discard the water and then cook it again in fresh water.

Edible and Useful Parts

Leaves and stalks: These can be eaten raw or cooked in salads and as a leafy green, or as a substitute for spinach or chard in any recipe. It's best to collect them young, and, as noted, it's a good idea not to eat a large quantity raw due to the high amounts of oxalic acid. They have a nice sour taste and can be used in salad dressings, pesto, omelets, or even in sweet creations as a rhubarb substitute.

Seeds: Wait until they are dry and brown to collect them. Rub off the papery brown part. Roast very lightly in a pan and grind into flour. The flour tastes similar to rye and makes great savory crackers, breads, and such. You can also soak the seeds for a few hours before roasting to remove some of the bitterness.

Roots: Roots can be used as a dye and for medicinal purposes.

Benefits: Dock is very high in iron and in vitamins A and C.

Sustainability: This plant is very widespread. Harvest with respect, but it is abundant and often considered a weed.

Dock Horta

This is a great simple recipe from Greece that can be used with many different wild greens. Horta was probably first made with foraged greens.

Ingredients
- Olive oil
- Lemon
- 5 cups wild young dock greens (or other wild greens), thoroughly washed. If your greens are older or you want to eat them regularly, you need to boil them in at least one change of water first.

Fry greens in olive oil with a bit of salt until they are wilted but not brown. Drizzle with more olive oil and lemon and serve as a side dish.

ELDERBERRY

Sambucus mexicana
Adoxaceae (Other common edible species in this family—viburnum)
Originates in North and South America and in Europe

—

A superhero of the edible plant world, elderberries are known for their many health benefits and their delicious flavor. The elder tree is thought by many cultures around the world to have magical powers; it is associated with fairies and mythical creatures and is used to make wands. Whether you are inclined to believe that or not, all can appreciate the beauty of blooming elders and the delicious taste of their immune-boosting fruit. I look forward to the elderberry harvest every year, and it is one of those wild edibles I will seek out and harvest in larger quantities.

Identification: Elderberry is a small to medium-size tree up to twenty-five feet tall, though usually much shorter. Its pinnate, opposite-branching leaves are easy to identify. Elders have dark-red or purple bumpy bark and fragile branches that are pithy inside. The flowers are abundant white clusters of tiny fragrant flowers. The berries are blue, often with a white powdery residue on top, and grow in large bunches. There are also red elderberries, though I rarely encounter them in the High Sierra. Those are only marginally edible and should be avoided. Although there are many varieties, blue and black elderberries can be used interchangeably. Some berries are sweeter than others, so experiment with your local variety.

Where to Find: Elderberries grow in partial shade in moist soils and near water, such as rivers and creeks.

When to Harvest: The flowers bloom in late June or July, and the berries are ripe in August or September.

How to Harvest: Just pull off the berries with your fingers when they are very ripe, or bring some scissors and cut off the clusters. Just remember to remove as much of the stems as you can before eating or preparing the berries. Remember to harvest with respect and give thanks to this special tree that many earth-based cultures considered sacred.

Poisonous Look-Alikes: Elderberry is an interesting plant in that it is both poisonous and edible. Many elderberries, especially unripe ones, are poisonous when eaten raw. They contain cyanide and toxic alkaloids. Blue and black elderberries can be eaten raw in small amounts, but if you are planning to consume large amounts, they need to be cooked before eating. There are reports of people juicing raw black or blue elderberries and getting poisoned.

There are actually many different types of elderberries—red, blue, and black—in the *Sambucus* genus. The red berries of *Sambucus racemosa*, for example, are more toxic than blue elderberries, and they always need to be properly cooked before eating. Although I know people who have eaten red elderberries, proceed with caution.

The flowers of the red elderberry are toxic as well. If you are harvesting elderberry flowers and don't know whether they are the red or the blue variety, one way to tell is that red elderberries often bloom earlier than blue ones. The trees are also often slightly smaller. But to be safe you might want to wait until they fruit. Fortunately, most of the elderberries in the northern Sierra are the blue or black kind.

Edible and Useful Parts

Flowers: Elderberry flowers can be used for tea, juice, jellies, wine, cordials, and fritters.

Berries: These sweet berries are very good for you and also very tasty. They make great juice, pies, jams, and other baked goods as well as wine and cordials. Elderberry juice and syrup taste great with a bit of cloves and cinnamon added to them and make a great cold-season gift. I also love to dry them and use them like little raisins. I freeze my elderberries before cooking, as this makes them sweeter. The berries can also be made into a beautiful pink or purple dye.

Other uses: With its unique pithy center that can be easily hollowed out, elder wood can be made into flutes, beads, containers, and instruments. It is also very good for making fire by friction.

Benefits: Elderberries are very good for you: they're high in antioxidants, vitamin C, and fiber. I use them for myself and my children as a tasty immune-boosting treat. We even make elderberry gummies ourselves with gelatin and elderberry syrup. Herbal medicine practitioners recommend elderberry for a variety of conditions and symptoms, but especially for coughs and colds.

Sustainability: Elderberries are quite abundant in many places. Leave them for wildlife wherever they are not as common, as birds love them. Because the edible parts are the fruit and flower, harvesting those parts of the tree in moderation is a sustainable practice. They are a great plant to grow in your yard. Please do not harvest elderberries, especially their wood, in Madera County, as there is an endangered wasp that lives in the trees and needs to be protected.

Swedish Elderblossom Juice

This is a favorite summer drink in Scandinavia. Kids love it, and many Scandinavians associate it with warm childhood memories.

Ingredients
- 20 elder blossom clusters
- 2 lemons
- 4½ cups water
- 5 cups sugar
- Optional: a few teaspoons of citric acid for preservation purposes

Cut the lemons and put them in a big jar. Wash and strain the elder flowers. Remove the main stems. Add them to the jar. Put in the citric acid if you are using it. Boil the water and pour it on the lemons and flowers. Cover and let steep in the fridge for 48 hours. Strain using a strainer or cheese cloth. Put the strained liquid in a pot and pour in the sugar. Bring to a boil and simmer for 5 minutes. Let it cool, then put it in bottles.

FERNS

Athyrium spp. and *Pteridium aquilinum*
Polypodiaceae
Originate throughout the world; lady fern originates in the United States
—

Ferns are members of a group of unique ancient plant families. They reproduce by spores rather than seeds. In some areas of the world, there are abundant edible species of ferns, and it is safe to eat those ferns raw or even to eat the leaves. When I traveled to New Zealand, for example, there were so many delicious, safe, edible ferns that I got a guidebook just on that topic. In the High Sierra, this is not the case. The key edible ferns here are lady ferns (*Athyrium* spp.) and Western bracken fern (*Pteridium aquilinum*). The ferns that grow in the High Sierra, like many ferns, contain carcinogens and toxic components in varying amounts and should be eaten only when young and cooked —and with caution. The young fiddleheads are delicious, however, and taste similar to asparagus.

Identification: Lady fern is a large, feathery plant two to five feet in height. The leaves are bright green; the stalks are green to purple or red. On the underside of the plant, the sori that produce the spores are horseshoe shaped.

Bracken fern is two to five feet high, with large, broad, triangular leaves growing from strong black horizontal root stalks.

Both ferns often grow in bunches with many together in the area.

Where to Find: Find ferns in clearings in wooded areas, in damp areas, and in areas of partial shade.

When to Harvest: Harvest ferns in spring.

How to Harvest: Look for the early fiddleheads and pick them gently.

Poisonous Look-Alikes: Some ferns could resemble poison hemlock with their feathery leaves, so make sure you can identify poison hemlock before harvesting ferns.

Caution: Bracken fern and lady fern both contain toxic components; eat only young, fully cooked plants, and in small amounts.

Edible and Useful Parts

Fiddleheads: These are young fern shoots. Harvest them only when they're very young and still furled so tightly that they're coiled up like little snakes. When the shoot unfurls, it's no longer good to eat. Boil them or fry them with a bit of butter and garlic.

Benefits: Fiddleheads are high in vitamins A and C.

Sustainability: I do not usually see large stands of fern in the High Sierra, so I harvest with caution.

Fern Fiddlehead Pasta

Fern fiddleheads suit a simple pasta very well. This is an easy-to-prepare meal with a wild twist.

Ingredients
- 1–2 cups fiddleheads
- Box of pasta of your choice
- Water
- Salt
- Butter
- Garlic

Prepare your favorite pasta. Make sure your fiddleheads are well washed and that all papery parts are removed. Sauté the fiddleheads in abundant butter, with salt and garlic. Toss them in with the pasta and mix. Serve right away.

FIREWEED

Chamerion angustifolium
Onagraceae (Other common edible species in this family—evening primrose)
Originates in northern temperate climates worldwide

———

Fireweed is another prolific edible plant often classified as a weed. Distributing its seeds through abundant wind-blown fluff, it is widespread around the world, often covering entire meadows. This plant gets its name from the fact that it easily blankets damaged areas in magenta or violet flowers. The taste of fireweed varies depending on what area it grows in. Here in the High Sierra, I have found it to be quite bitter unless picked very young. Regardless, it is an easy wild edible to forage, especially in the aftermath of wildfire.

Identification: Fireweed is a tall, slender perennial plant up to six feet tall, with alternating lanceolate leaves that have a clear central vein that is usually white. The underside of the leaf also has a circular pattern of veins, and the veins do not extend all the way to the edge of the leaf. A spike of abundant magenta or violet flowers grows from the hard, almost woody stem. The seeds are woolly and tufted like thistledown.

Where to Find: Look for fireweed in disturbed places, meadows, and moist areas.

When to Harvest: Harvest this plant in spring and summer.

How to Harvest: Pinch off the flowers and leaves, or cut the stem.

Poisonous Look-Alikes: A flowering fireweed is hard to mistake, but a young plant could resemble toxic lily-family plants. I suggest starting with flowering fireweed and getting to know the leaves. Once you can recognize the leaf vein pattern well, you will be able to safely harvest younger plants.

Edible and Useful Parts

Leaves: The leaves are best harvested when young. Just pinch some off carefully; that way you can leave the flowers for the bees that love them. The leaves can be eaten cooked or raw as a green. They can also be dried and used for tea.

Flowers: The flowers of fireweed are a favorite of pollinators and make a wonderful honey. They can also be made into jellies and drinks or used as decoration.

Seeds: The fluffy seeds can be used as tinder for fire making or to stuff a pillow.

Stems: Use these when they first shoot up in the spring. Pinch off the stem when young or, when it's older, cut it off with scissors or a knife and peel it. It can be cooked or eaten raw much as you would an asparagus.

Once the stem gets tough, it's also possible to cut it open and just eat the inside.

Roots: The roots are a medicinal anti-inflammatory.

Benefits: Fireweed is high in vitamin C and is used as an anti-inflammatory.

Sustainability: Fireweed is very abundant; harvest it in places where that is the case.

Fireweed Pizza

This pizza is also good with a wild-green pesto sauce, such as thistle pesto, instead of tomato sauce.

Ingredients
- Pizza dough or base (use your favorite recipe or premade dough)
- Tomato sauce (jarred or homemade)
- Cup or so of young fireweed stalks, washed and sliced
- Mushrooms
- Wild or store-bought greens, washed and chopped finely
- Olive oil
- Salt
- Pepper
- Grated cheese of your choice (optional)

Preheat oven to 350°. Prepare the pizza dough according to your recipe or the packaged dough's instructions. You can add ground dock seeds into your pizza dough for a wild twist! Spread a thin layer of tomato sauce on the dough. Put toppings on the sauce. Drizzle with olive oil and add a pinch of salt and pepper. Cover with a thin layer of grated cheese if desired. Put in the oven and cook for approximately 20 minutes or until the cheese bubbles. Enjoy with a wild green salad.

HORSETAILS

Equisetum spp.
Equisetaceae
Originate in temperate regions of the Northern Hemisphere
—

When I see horsetail growing by the Truckee River or in a mountain meadow, I feel a sense of joy, familiarity, and awe. When I was little, my grandmother would take me on forest walks and teach me about plants. When we found a horsetail, she would always tell me that it was a big tree in the age of the dinosaurs and then shrank. Horsetails are indeed ancient plants considered to be "living fossils" from the Devonian period approximately 350 million years ago. They grew thick as forests and had relatives that were as big as trees. So when you sample some horsetail tea, you are experiencing an ancient taste. They are quite common in the Sierra, so you should not have any trouble sharing this dinosaur tree with any kids on a hike and even brushing your teeth with its fibrous stem.

Identification: Horsetails are low-growing perennial plants with hollow, sometimes evergreen stems. Some horsetails, such as the common horsetail, have needle-like segmented leaves that wrap around the stem in a whorl. It looks like a large green bottlebrush, which is why it is called that sometimes. The stems and leaves have clear segments that sometimes turn dark at the joints and are rough to the touch. These ancient plants have spores that are produced in cone-like structures at the top instead of seeds. There are three main types of horsetail in the Sierra: common horsetail (*E. arvense*), smooth scouring rush (*E. laevigatum*), and common scouring rush (*E. hyemale*). I believe that what I say here applies to all of them, but I only have personal experience eating common horsetail (*E. arvense*).

Where to Find: Find horsetail in wet areas—by rivers, creeks, and wet meadows.

When to Harvest: Horsetail can be harvested from spring to fall.

How to Harvest: Pinch off the desired part gently.

Poisonous Look-Alikes: There are none that I know of.

Edible and Useful Parts

Stems and leaves: The stems and leaves of horsetail can be dried for use as a tea. The flavor is pleasant and soft, in my opinion, though I usually include other herbs as well, as noted in the recipe I've included here.

Other uses: Horsetail stems can also be used like sandpaper due to their rough consistency. They also make a "wild" toothbrush, as they are high in silica and can be good for scrubbing.

Benefits: Horsetail is very high in minerals, especially silica and silicone. It is therefore reputed to help strengthen bones and hair. Horsetail has been used medicinally to address many conditions, especially those resulting from mineral deficiency. However, consuming horsetail very regularly is not recommended—although it offers some benefits, it also contains an enzyme that can create a thiamine deficiency if eaten too often.

Sustainability: Horsetail is often considered an invasive weed. Just follow the rules for conscious harvesting outlined earlier in this book.

Mia's Mountain Mineral Tea

This tea is very good for strength and for those who are trying to increase the amount of minerals in their body. A note of warning: nettles are diuretic and may make you pee a lot. If that's undesirable, you can leave them out.

Ingredients

Handful of each of the following dried herbs:
- Horsetail
- Nettle
- Oat straw
- Blackberry, raspberry, or currant leaf
- Wild mint (for flavor)

Boil some water. Put the herbs in a pint-size Ball jar. Pour boiling water over them, close the lid, and let steep for 10–20 minutes.

INCENSE CEDAR

Calocedrus decurrens
Cupressaceae (Other common edible species in this family—cypress)
Originates in northwestern America

—

Even though incense cedar is not commonly eaten, I could not write about
Sierra Nevada plants without including this revered tree with many medicinal, practical, and spiritual uses and a long, meaningful local history. Even if
I use incense cedar just as a flavoring or garnish, its earthy, pungent fragrance
and flavor are essential for me in creating the taste of the region. With that
said, I only harvest these sacred trees with great consideration. I feel so much
respect and gratitude for the cedar trees of the Sierra. Their aromatic, cleansing fragrance fills the air, and the beauty of their form inspires many local
artists. I doubt there will ever be a time that I come upon a Sierra cedar that
has been struck by lightning and am not filled with awe. Just being around
them feels nourishing to me.

Identification: These tall trees reach
heights of 75–125 feet. Cedars have
reddish, deeply textured, shedding
bark. The leaves are scaly and branch
in a finger-like fashion. They have
an aromatic smell. When walking
in a coniferous forest in the Sierra,
look for the trees that have a lighter-
colored, more variable bark than
the pines and firs, and branches that
grow in more directions and with
more character. The larger ones often
have neon-green wolf lichen growing
on them. Once you learn to distin-
guish cedars from pines, you will
be able to spot a cedar from a long
distance.

Where to Find: Cedars grow at
elevations of 6,000–8,000 feet. They
are very common in Sierra forests,
ideally in acidic sandy loam.

When to Harvest: They can be harvested all year round.

How to Harvest: Please harvest with
great respect. Cut or pinch off leaves
or harvest freshly fallen ones off
the ground.

Poisonous Look-Alikes: There
are none that I know of in the
High Sierra.

Caution: Pregnant or breastfeeding
women should not use cedar.

Edible and Useful Parts

There are so many uses for cedar
trees that entire books have been
written on the subject. All parts of
the tree are useful.

Leaves: The leaves of cedar can
be used for flavoring in a calming
tea and in meat and fish dishes or
barbecues. They can also be used to
preserve and flavor acorns, as they
are antimicrobial. Medicinally they
can be made into tea or a tincture,
sprinkled into a bath, or distilled into

an essential oil. One of my favorite uses of cedar leaves is to burn them as an incense. I also like putting them in baking soda to make an antimicrobial foot powder for shoes.

Other uses: Cedar bark and wood have a myriad of uses. To highlight a few, they can be made into baskets, boats, and shelters. Cedar is one of the woods I most prefer for making a fire by friction using a bow drill kit. Shredded cedar bark can also be good tinder.

Benefits: Cedar is highly medicinal and has been used for colds, respiratory conditions, stress relief, toenail fungus, and more. Cedar is also antifungal and antimicrobial and can help in food preservation.

Sustainability: Incense cedars are very common in the Sierra, and materials can often be harvested from fallen branches. Please harvest with respect.

Barbecued Cedar Fish

Many people use cedar planks to flavor fish and meat. Here is a way to imbue your food with a unique mountain taste without needing to cut down a tree.

Ingredients
- Fish of your choice
- A few cedar sprigs per fish
- A few slices of lemon per fish
- Salt and pepper to taste

Wrap fish in aluminum foil with cedar sprigs, lemon, salt, and pepper. Place on hot coals in a fire or on a barbecue grill and cook until done. Serve with fresh wild salad.

JUNIPERS

Juniperus spp.
Cupressaceae (Other common edible species in this family—cypress)
Originate in the northwestern United States
—

If I was going to cook up a pot of Sierra stew, juniper would definitely need to be included. It is an essential part of tasting the Sierra, especially getting the Eastern Sierra flavor. Junipers define the landscape in drier areas of the Sierra, and I often stop to admire their varied, weather-beaten, artistic shapes on my hikes. I love picking a few berries off of these special little trees on a high-desert hike and simply chewing on them while I walk, or placing them in my water bottle for flavor. The bitter but foresty flavor gives me that extra zing to keep going and connects me with my landscape.

Identification: These evergreen trees or shrubs range from four to fifty feet tall. Most of them are around six to ten feet. The leaves are scaly and needle-like, spreading like fingers. The bark is light brown and full of character. The male cones are small; the female cones are larger and like berries. The berries have little triangular ridges that come to a point; they ripen to a bluish purple color and often have a bit of a white waxy covering. There are two main types of junipers in the High Sierra: dwarf juniper (*J. communis*) and mountain juniper (*J. occidentalis*), both of which offer that special Sierra flavor.

Where to Find: Juniper can be found in dry habitats both in high desert and on rocky slopes.

When to Harvest: Harvest juniper in late summer and fall.

How to Harvest: Pick berries when ripe; you can harvest twigs anytime.

Poisonous Look-Alikes: There are none that I know of.

Caution: Eating fresh juniper leaves in large quantities is not recommended.

Edible and Useful Parts

Twigs: These can be dried for tea and seasoning.

Cones: Cones can be eaten raw, but it's better to dry them and make them into a flour that you can use in breads or crackers.

Berries: These can be eaten raw, dried, or roasted. They are good for seasoning or smoking meats, making tea, or flavoring beverages and foods. Gin is made by flavoring grain alcohol with juniper berries.

Other uses: The bark is useful for tinder and fire making.

Benefits: Juniper berries are used for urinary health problems, for detoxifying, and for promoting digestive health. They are antibacterial and protect against infection. An essential oil is often made with juniper berries.

Sustainability: Junipers are very common in the Sierra.

Easy Choucroute Garnie

This traditional German recipe is flavored with juniper berries and is a good winter mountain meal after a long day in the snow. I like it because it incorporates healthy sauerkraut in an unusual way.

Ingredients
- 2 tablespoons oil
- 1 pound sausage, ideally smoked (vegan is fine)
- 1 onion, chopped
- 1 teaspoon caraway seeds
- 10 dried juniper berries, ground, with seeds removed
- 1 pound sauerkraut, drained
- $2/3$ cup broth or white wine

Chop the sausage and fry in the oil. Add onions. Add the rest of the ingredients and let simmer for about 10–15 minutes. Add salt and pepper to taste. Serve with potatoes if desired.

LAMB'S QUARTERS

Chenopodium spp.
Amaranthaceae (Other common edible species in this family—
    spinach, amaranth)
Originate in Europe and the United States

___

Lamb's quarters is a widespread wild edible that is easy to identify and has a mild, palatable taste. It is a generous food plant that can be used much like spinach and is therefore a good fit for even a beginner forager. It is mostly found near human habitation here in the Sierra. I enjoy snacking on the leaves as I see them or using them as a side-dish green.

Identification: Lamb's quarters is a low-growing plant up to three feet tall with uniquely shaped triangular leaves that grow alternating on the stem. The name of the genus comes from the Greek words *chen* (goose) and *podion* (little foot). Lamb's quarters is easy to identify by the shape of its leaves and the shiny white powder they have on the underside. The upper leaves are smaller and look dusty because they are covered in tiny white hairs. This plant can occasionally have a purple hue depending on the soil it grows in. The flowers are small and look like miniature green popcorn. The seeds are brown and in clusters. There are multiple species of *Chenopodium* in the High Sierra, and they are all edible, though generally the ones with larger leaves tend to taste better.

Where to Find: Lamb's quarters grows in waste places, disturbed sites, weedy meadows, and sidewalk cracks.

When to Harvest: Harvest lamb's quarters from spring to fall.

How to Harvest: Pinch off a whole leaf cluster right above a joint. Pick older leaves individually. Pull seeds into your hand.

Poisonous Look-Alikes: Black nightshade can look similar to this plant, but is rarely found in the High Sierra. For certain identification of lamb's quarters, make sure the triangular leaf shape and white shiny powder are present.

Caution: Because raw *Chenopodium* is high in oxalic acid, eating large quantities is not recommended. Cooking reduces the amount of oxalic acid, so I recommend that you boil, fry, or steam your lamb's quarters if you want to make a full meal of it.

Edible and Useful Parts

Leaves: These can be eaten like spinach, raw and cooked. Use them in soups and stews, and as a side green much like chard, which, incidentally, is in the same family. Younger leaves on plants under a foot tall are best. Older leaves can still be eaten, but should be picked without the stem and may have a more bitter taste.

Seeds: Wait until they mature and then rub them between your hands to separate husk from tiny seed. They can be roasted and used in baking or cereals. I have heard that the seeds can also be popped like amaranth and corn, but I have not tried this myself.

Benefits: *Chenopodium* species are high in vitamin A and calcium.

Sustainability: *Chenopodium alba* is considered a noxious weed in most places, and there does not tend to be a concern about the native species.

Quick-and-Easy Wild Lamb's Quarters "Saagish"

This is one of my favorite recipes. It is inspired by the Indian dish *saag paneer* or *saag aloo*, but I call it saag*ish*, as it's my own interpretation. It's a great way to incorporate just about any wild green.

All greens should be thoroughly washed so that they don't bring dust and sand into the dish.

Ingredients
- Bunch of lamb's quarters greens, chopped; young stems and even young flower heads are fine
- Bunch of other greens, such as nettle, dock leaves, blackberry or raspberry leaves, or wild mustard leaves—any mix and quantity is fine
- Enough spinach to compensate for any lack of wild greens and to soften the flavor
- Butter or vegan butter
- ½–1 cup broth or water
- ⅓ cup nondairy milk or dairy cream
- 1 onion, chopped
- 2 tablespoons ginger
- Curry paste to taste—about 2–5 tablespoons depending on your taste and type of curry paste you use

Fry the onion in butter or oil until translucent. Add the greens and fry until wilted but not brown. Add a bit of broth or water and the cream or nondairy milk. You want enough moisture to make a sauce, but the amount of liquid you add will depend on how watery your greens were. Add the ginger and the curry paste and some salt to taste. You can also add a choice of cooked meat, paneer, or cubed cooked potatoes. Simmer for 5–10 minutes and serve with rice.

MANZANITAS

Arctostaphylos spp.

Ericaceae (Other common edible species in this family—huckleberries, blueberries, cranberries, uva-ursi, rhododendrons)
Originate in Northern California

—

Manzanita is one of the first edible plants I learned about in California. I was hiking near Lake Tahoe with a friend, up in the high sunny hills on a hot day, and he told me that if you chew on the leaves of a manzanita, they help keep you from getting dehydrated. I was delighted to learn about an edible plant native to my adopted home. Although it is true that manzanita leaves stimulate saliva because they are astringent, I doubt that they actually restore hydration, as they are quite dry. Putting a few in your water bottle, however, or drinking a tea made from the leaves is refreshing. Many years later, I thank manzanita, and my friend, who helped me realize on that hike that indeed there were many edible plants in this region.

Manzanitas are not only useful and edible plants but also beautiful, with smooth reddish bark and unique shapes. They define the California landscape for me. I enjoy traveling through California, sampling the slightly different manzanita tastes of each region. Manzanitas are very abundant in the Sierra. Sometimes the fruits tend to be a bit on the small side, especially compared to the berries that grow in wetter areas, such as Mendocino County. *Manzanita* is the word for "little apple" in Spanish, and sure enough, these little Sierra treats taste like Granny Smith apples when they are not quite ripe and even sweeter when they fully ripen. Their texture is mealy, which confuses some people who are used to juicier berries, but once you get past that, their flavor is really delightful.

Identification: Manzanitas are perennial shrubs about three to six feet tall in the Sierra, though they can grow to twenty feet tall in other areas of California. They have beautiful smooth mahogany bark that peels in papery sheets. The leaves are oval, quite thick and smooth. The flowers are pink or white and urn shaped. The common manzanita species in the High Sierra are greenleaf manzanita (*A. patula*), pinemat manzanita (*A. nevadensis*), and bearberry (*A. uva-ursi*).

Where to Find: Find manzanita on sunny rocky slopes and in open forest; it prefers sandy acidic soils.

When to Harvest: Harvest in summer and fall.

How to Harvest: Pinch off the desired part gently.

Poisonous Look-Alikes: Not all red berries are edible, so be sure to look for manzanita's dark-red bark to make a clear identification.

Edible and Useful Parts

Leaves: You can chew on the leaves or make them into a tea. They can also be dried and used in smoke blends.

Flowers: Eat them as is or use them to decorate a dish. Insects love these flowers too, so take just a few.

Berries: Manzanita berries can be eaten raw or cooked. Wait until they are orangey-red and dry. Then gather them and eat them as is, or grind them into a powder using a mortar and pestle, and pass it through a sieve to remove the seeds. The powder can be used like sugar; added to smoothies, ice cream, or cereals; or made into a drink by adding water.

Seeds: Some people use these as a base for a cider, but I have not tried this myself. I usually spit them out in the landscape and hope they will grow.

Bark: Crushed bark can be made into an earthy tea.

Benefits: Manzanitas and most of the *Ericaceae* family have been commonly used to treat urinary tract infections and stomachaches.

Sustainability: Manzanitas are very common native plants, but please always follow the conscious harvesting guidelines. They are a beautiful native plant to grow in your yard as well, and will attract many types of beneficial insects, such as bees and butterflies.

Manzanita Muffins

This is a nice late-summer treat. You can add any other processed wild berries to it as well—for example, thimbleberries, currants, or even de-seeded rose hips.

Ingredients

- ⅓ cup coconut oil
- ¼ cup sweetener of your choice
- 2 eggs or egg replacement
- Zest of 1 orange
- 3 cups manzanita berries
- 1 cup thick yogurt or nondairy yogurt
- 1¾ cup flour of your choice
- ½ teaspoon salt
- 1 teaspoon baking powder

Grind manzanita berries using a mortar and pestle. Pass through a sieve to remove seeds. Preheat oven to 350°. Grease muffin tins. Melt coconut oil. Mix together with sweetener, eggs, orange zest, berries, and yogurt until blended. Add flour, salt, and baking powder, and mix to blend. Pour mixture into muffin tins and bake for 20–25 minutes. Frost with your favorite frosting if desired. Sprinkle with manzanita sugar (powdered seeds).

Missing Manzanita Berries

Every year, I look forward to late summer when the manzanita berries finally ripen. I enjoy nibbling on them as a seasonal treat when I'm on a hike. I watch the flowers and green berries and find joy in witnessing their growth every year. Sometimes I nibble on those too, but the fully ripe berries are really the best. Just as I do every year, I watched this progression from flower to berry in 2021, with great anticipation of one of my favorite tastes of the Sierra. There were plenty of beautiful flowers in late spring and early summer. I looked forward to enjoying the berries. But then something strange happened, something I had never seen before. When it came time for the ripe berries, there were almost none. The ones that were there were tiny and didn't taste good. The same actually happened with the gooseberries. They were tiny and shrunken or not present at all. I was and am concerned about the health of these precious plants. Last year was a significant drought year and very hot at times, but I've witnessed manzanitas deal with serious drought conditions, so I was surprised. Could the manzanitas have been affected by the fires? I doubt it. Their seeds actually need fire to germinate. Did the bears eat them all really quickly? I know they love them. And why did the rose hips ripen just fine when the manzanitas, gooseberries, and thimbleberries did not? Mysterious. I'm hoping the berries will return this year. I was quite disturbed by their absence for many months. Should anyone else have any information about the missing manzanita berries in the autumn of 2021, please feel free to contact me.

MOUNTAIN ASH

Sorbus spp.
Rosaceae (Other common edible species in this family—roses, apples,
   strawberries, raspberries)
Originate in North America, Europe, and Asia

———

One of my favorite trees growing up in Finland was a leaning rowan (*Sorbus
aucuparia*) tree that I spent many hours sitting in. My grandpa would perpet-
ually threaten to cut it down, as it obstructed his view of the sea, but we kids
would vehemently oppose him every time. It continues to amaze me just how
deep and significant childhood connections to nature are. When I moved
to the Sierra, I was happy to see another species of the beautiful red-berried
mountain ash growing here. I have not heard of anyone here eating mountain ash berries, but they are edible, though slightly bitter. They do make a
nice jelly, however, with a unique flavor that pairs well with meat and fish
and could be a great feature in a special dish. I grew up eating a jelly candy
made with rowan berries and also would frequently crush them with my
friends into a beautiful orange-colored drink that we rarely drank much of but
enjoyed making.

Identification: Mountain ash is a
deciduous perennial tree ten to thirty
feet tall. It is easily identified by
its compound leaves with serrated
edges. Its flowers are white, and its
red-orange berries grow in beautiful
bunches. The bark is gray, often with
whitish spots. There are two native
species in the High Sierra, and I
suspect another planted nonnative
species. The two common native species are California mountain ash (*S.
californica*) and western mountain
ash (*S. scopulina*).

Where to Find: Ash is often planted
in suburban areas and also can be
found in forest openings and moist
meadows.

When to Harvest: Wait until the
berries are fully ripe—most likely
late fall. They are often tastier after
the first frost.

How to Harvest: Pick the bunches of
berries.

Poisonous Look-Alikes: Mountain
ash berries resemble red elderberries
quite a bit, but are red and ripe in late
fall, a long time after red elderberries
are already gone. The bark of the
two trees is also distinctly different.
Mountain ash bark is smooth and
gray. There also are not that many red
elderberries in the Sierra.

Edible and Useful Parts

Flowers: Sprinkle the flowers
on salads.

Berries: You can eat these berries raw
in small amounts, but they are ideally
cooked or dried. They can be used
to flavor drinks, desserts, jams, and
jellies. They are high in pectin and
therefore gel easily. They can also be
cooked with meat and used in savory

dishes, such as soup. The berries also make a really nice orange-red natural dye.

Benefits: Mountain ash berries are high in vitamin C.

Sustainability: The berries are abundant, and though many birds like them, they tend to just rot on the branches. Mountain ash is a beautiful landscaping plant providing white fragrant flowers in the early summer, gorgeous red berry bunches in the fall into winter, and very colorful fall leaves. I highly recommend planting them in your Sierra yard.

Mountain Ash Jelly

This jelly pairs well with game meat or a sharp cheese.

Ingredients
- 1 pound sugar
- 5 pounds mountain ash berries
- 2 pounds apples

Remove stems from rowan berries and wash. Core the apples. Put the berries and apples in a large pot. Cover with water. Bring to a rolling boil. Simmer for 20–30 minutes or until the fruit is soft. Let cool, and pour the fruit and water in a jelly strainer bag suspended for at least 12 hours over a bowl or pot. Add 1 pound of sugar for every 2 cups of strained juice into the pot. Bring to a boil and stir so the sugar dissolves. Heat until the liquid looks gelatinous. Test the consistency with a spoon; continue to heat until the jelly doesn't drop off the spoon but rather sticks to it. If you're having trouble, you can refer to the many canning guides available for more specific guidance on making fruit jellies. Pour into sterilized jars and place in the fridge to set. Well preserved, the jelly is shelf-stable and should keep for at least a year.

MOUNTAIN COYOTE MINT

Monardella odoratissima
Lamiaceae
Originates on the West Coast of North America

—

A little blue butterfly showed me my first coyote mint blossoms of the season this year. The butterflies and bees love this plant with its easy-to-access flower and sweet scent, and following the pollinators will often help you find it. It is very common in coniferous forest openings. Once you see one of these plants, you will suddenly see it everywhere.

There is something so comforting about finding wild mint. It is familiar and easy to identify, smells so sweet, and tastes so good. There are many different species of wild mint as well as feral mints in the Sierra. The common name coyote mint can apply to several different plants. Here I am particularly referring to *M. odoratissima*, which is also sometimes called mountain pennyroyal. I don't like using the pennyroyal name, as pennyroyal to me is a water-loving plant with a very intense flavor, whereas this coyote mint grows in fairly dry, sandy places and tastes much softer. Pennyroyal is also in the *Mentha* genus, not *Monardella*.

Identification: Mountain coyote mint is a fairly inconspicuous bunching, low-growing plant about one foot tall, with small, oval, smooth, opposite-branching leaves. The mint (Lamiaceae) family in general, of which most are edible, can be identified by a square stem, opposite leaves, and aromatic odor. This plant can be quite easy to miss until it shoots out tall flower stalks with puffball-shaped white or lilac flowers. You don't have to wait until it flowers to identify it, though, because if you smell a leaf, it should clearly smell like mint. That's what is so wonderfully easy about the mint family: there are no other plants I know of that smell like that, and most of us know what mint smells like. Of course the smell of wild mints is slightly different and usually softer than cultivated ones, but definitely recognizable.

Where to Find: Find mountain coyote mint in mountain meadows near coniferous forests, in sun or partial shade.

When to Harvest: Harvest this plant in late spring and summer.

How to Harvest: It's best to harvest this plant before it flowers; pinch off a piece on the stem just a bit above any two-leaf pair anywhere toward the top, or just take a few leaves separately.

Poisonous Look-Alikes: There are no poisonous plants that smell like mint. Pennyroyal is a strong mint that, though not poisonous, should not be eaten by children or pregnant women, as it is strongly medicinal. Pennyroyal is usually found in clearly wet areas; it has purple flowers and a much stronger scent than mountain coyote mint.

Leaves: All parts of mints are edible, though the leaves are most commonly used, either fresh or dried (and made into tea). One of my favorite ways to eat this plant is to put a few leaves of it in my water bottle while hiking to make an instant mint tea. You can also just chew on a few leaves. Of course you could collect more, but harvesting a lot of a delicate mountain plant just doesn't feel right to me most of the time. So unless I'm on a lightweight camping trip where I need supplementation from wild foods, I would probably just sample a few sweet pieces.

Flowers: These can be beautiful and delicious as well.

Benefits: Mints are generally good for digestion and colds. They are invigorating yet also calming in nature.

Sustainability: Coyote mint is quite common, but it's a native plant and so should be harvested sparingly. With that said, if harvested with caution, mints regenerate quite easily.

Mountain Mint Ice Cream

This makes a wonderful cold treat for a summer day. Wild mint has a very soft flavor, different from what you may be used to in regular mint ice cream. You need to use quite a bit to get the flavor to show up.

Ingredients
- 1 cup cream
- 1 cup milk
- ½ cup sugar
- 1 cup wild mint

Crush mint leaves. Add sugar and mix well. Add milk and cream. Refrigerate for 1–2 hours so that mint flavor seeps in. Prepare in an ice cream maker or use your preferred method for making ice cream.

MUGWORT

Artemisia douglasiana
Asteraceae (Other common edible species in this family—daisies, artichokes, dandelions, thistles, sunflowers)
Originates in Europe and Asia

___

Mugwort is a highly medicinal plant considered sacred by many cultures. California mugwort (*Artemisia douglasiana*) is closely related to common mugwort (*Artemisia vulgaris*), a species native to Europe and Asia, where it has a long history—from being made into mugwort beer, which used to be very common, to being used as moxa to gently heat acupuncture points in Chinese medicine. The name "mugwort" may have come from its popular use in the Middle Ages for beer flavoring or for sanitizing beer mugs. It is also known as an herb that enhances dreams.

Identification: Mugwort is a low-growing aromatic herbaceous plant two to six feet tall. It has a sturdy, almost woody stem and forked leaves that get smaller as they ascend. The leaves are green and smooth on top and whitish and a bit hairy underneath. Mugwort flowers are numerous, pinkish or yellowish white, small, and quite nondescript. The plant often grows in patches. Mugwort has a strong, fragrant smell, which is an easy way to identify it if you are not sure.

Where to Find: You can look for mugwort at the edges of woods or along disturbed trails in full or partial sun. It is a hardy plant and can tolerate a variety of conditions.

When to Harvest: Harvest mugwort in spring and summer.

How to Harvest: Pinch off the top sprigs before they flower or take a few leaves.

Poisonous Look-Alikes: There are none that I know of.

Caution: Pregnant women should not eat mugwort, as it stimulates blood flow around the uterus.

Edible and Useful Parts

Leaves: The leaves are usually used cooked. They have a strong flavor and are very medicinal, so they are best eaten in moderation as flavoring. Monks have cooked mugwort as a vegetable with rice as their ceremonial fasting meal. If you want to explore more uses of mugwort, there are a lot of Asian cooking traditions that you can refer to online, ranging from mugwort mochi to mugwort soups. My favorite way to use mugwort leaves is as a tinder bundle when I make a fire by friction. It is an excellent and fragrant way to catch the coal on fire. I also love using the leaves as moxa and find it very healing.

Benefits: There are various benefits to mugwort, which is rich in vitamin K and folate. Many people enjoy its benefits to both mental and physical health.

Sustainability: Mugwort is quite common and hardy and can be sustainably harvested when you only take the tips or just a few leaves, as they will regrow. It is also a sacred plant, especially in its places of origin, so I recommend harvesting with respect and remembering to say thank you. Mugwort is a great plant to grow in your garden.

Monk-Like Mugwort Rice

Ingredients
- 1 cup mugwort
- 2 cups rice
- Water
- Salt
- Pepper

Cook the rice using your preferred method. Boil the mugwort leaves in salted water for about 8 minutes. Crush the cooked leaves with a food processor and add salt and pepper to taste. Mix the rice and mugwort and enjoy as a very simple medicinal meal. Alternatively, you can make it fancier by adding seaweed, carrots, shiitake mushrooms, sesame seeds, and some soy sauce or ponzu sauce.

MULLEIN

Verbascum thapsus
Scrophulariaceae (Other common edible species in this
family—snapdragons)
Originates in Europe, North Africa, and western Asia

___

It's hard to imagine a time that mullein was not part of the Sierra landscape. It is such a prominent and easy-to-spot plant now, towering over most other low-growing plants. Since settlers brought it to these mountains, it has become emblematic of the area. Of course, with its numerous medicinal uses, it's not surprising that mullein accompanied those who moved to the Sierra Nevada many years ago. Mullein's edible uses are a bit limited, but it is a highly medicinal plant, and has helped ease my dry cough many a time. I like to collect its tall stalks in the early fall when they are dry and save them for use in the winter as hand drills in making fire by friction. (No one should be making fires in the Sierra in the fall, of course—the season is too dry and the wildfire danger too high.) Mullein has a mild, fragrant flavor, and you can eat its tender leaves and stalk.

Identification: Mullein is a biannual plant that grows up to six feet high, with large, soft, woolly leaves. It starts as a large basal rosette and then shoots up a long stalk topped by a large flower head in its second year. The flowers are abundant, small, and yellow, and they flower for a long time.

Where to Find: You can find mullein in meadows and disturbed places; it grows well after fires.

When to Harvest: Harvest this plant in early summer.

How to Harvest: You can pinch off young leaves or cut the last six to eight inches of the early flower stalk.

Poisonous Look-Alikes: There are none to my knowledge. Mule's ears do look a bit like mullein because of their woolly leaves, but they don't have the same flower stalk.

Edible and Useful Parts

Leaves: The leaves can be used for a tea or steam that soothes the lungs. Very young leaves can be cooked and eaten in small quantities, though the hairy texture is unpleasant. People also use the leaves in smoke blends. The leaves can be used as toilet paper, though the little hairs can be slightly irritating.

Young flower stalks: The top of the young flower stalk can be cut and then peeled and cooked like asparagus.

Other uses: The dry stalks can be used for fire making.

Benefits: Mullein helps promote lung health.

Sustainability: Mullein is very common and considered an invasive weed.

Mullein Tea

This tea tastes pleasant and can be very helpful for a dry cough.

Ingredients
- A few dried mullein leaves and/or flowers
- Water
- Ball jar
- Honey (optional)

Place dried mullein leaves and flowers in the Ball jar and pour boiling water over them, just enough to cover. Close the lid and steep for 10 minutes. Add honey to taste.

MUSTARDS, CRESSES, AND RADISHES

Brassica spp., Nasturtium spp., Raphanus spp.
Brassicaceae (Other common edible species in this family—kale, broccoli, cauliflower)
Originate in various places

___

There are several different species of mustards, radishes, and cresses in the Sierra. They are all similar in terms of edibility, which is why I decided to cover them together. Most members of the Brassicaceae family are edible, so if you see a symmetrical cross-shaped, four-petaled flower with long, thin green seedpods and alternate leaves, you're in luck. They all taste spicy and can be used fairly interchangeably. The most common species in the High Sierra are yellowrocket (*Barbarea vulgaris*), rock cress (*Aubrieta deltoidea*), black mustard (*Brassica nigra*), shepherd's purse (*Capsella bursa-pastoris*), Western wallflower (*Erysimum capitatum*), bittercress (*Cardamine hirsuta*), peppergrass (*Lepidium virginicum*), and watercress (*Nasturtium officinale*). (There are also six different hedge mustards [*Sisymbrium* spp.] in California.) Some of these various plants can be too bitter to eat, so just sample to see whether what you've found is palatable.

Identification: Members of the Brassicaceae family are annual or perennial herbaceous plants up to two and a half feet tall. They have long, slender stems and alternating leaves that are often forked. The best identifying characteristic is the four-petaled flowers, which can be yellow, purple, or white. They are in the shape of a cross, with six stamens: four long and two short.

Where to Find: Plants of the Brassicaceae family can be found in various habitats from wet to dry, often in meadows or on the edges of human habitation.

When to Harvest: Harvest these plants in spring and summer.

How to Harvest: Harvest by simply by pinching off the desired part.

Poisonous Look-Alikes: Most members of the *Brassica* genus are easy to identify if you wait until their flowering stage. Be careful not to harvest watercress before it flowers unless you really know it, as the young leaves can easily resemble those of water hemlock.

Edible and Useful Parts

Leaves: You can eat the leaves raw or cooked, in salads, soups, and stews.

Flowers: Use the flowers raw as a decoration in salads or for snacking on.

Seedpods: The pods are spicy and radish-like; eat them before they get too dry.

Seeds: Seeds can be used as a spice or ground into a flour mix.

Roots: The roots can be eaten raw or cooked, as you would a radish or horseradish.

<u>Benefits:</u> Members of the Brassicaceae family are high in vitamins K and C and in omega 3s.

<u>Sustainability:</u> Many *Brassica* species, such as common wild mustard and radish, are very prolific and even invasive. Others are native and more rare. Harvest those that are in abundance.

Wild Mustard Noodle Soup

This is an easy, nourishing meal to make; you can even pack it in a thermos for a picnic lunch on a hike. The rice noodles can be placed in the thermos and will cook while you hike.

Ingredients
- 1 cup mustard, cress, or radish greens, washed well and chopped
- 2 cups bone or vegetable broth
- 1 tablespoon fresh ginger, grated
- 2 garlic cloves, pressed
- Packet of tofu (optional)
- 2 tablespoons soy sauce or to taste
- Packet of rice noodles

Heat broth with spices. Add tofu and noodles and simmer. Add greens. Serve with some rice crackers.

OREGON GRAPE

Berberis aquifolium
Berberidaceae (Other common edible species in this family—barberries)
Originates in western North America
—

This plant is so shiny leaved and spiky that it took me a while to believe that the purple berries were actually edible, especially since I often find it in landscaping at vacation condos. Shade-tolerant landscaping plants are often not edible, so I was surprised. I find the fresh-picked berries to be sweet, but they sometimes have a bitter taste that I don't always enjoy. But cooked and with a bit of sweetener added, they are quite delicious. Oregon grapes are well known and revered for their medicinal properties. They are common in the High Sierra and easy to spot, as the bright-yellow flowers stand out against the dark-green foliage. There are two main species in the Sierra: barberry (*B. nervosa*) and Oregon grape (*B. aquifolium*), both of which can be used in the same way.

Identification: Oregon grape is an evergreen shrub growing up to ten feet tall, though usually more like four feet in the Sierra. The leaves are shiny, stiff, and serrated with spikes, reminiscent of a holly. The fruits are bluish purple and have a waxy covering much like table grapes. They can be low growing and trailing, or upright.

Where to Find: Look for Oregon grape in shady areas, rocky woods, coniferous forests, and landscaping.

When to Harvest: Harvest this plant in summer.

How to Harvest: Pinch off the berries and watch out for the spiked leaves.

Poisonous Look-Alikes: There are none that I know of.

Cautions: Some reports say to exercise caution with the leaves, which can inject fungus into the skin. Oregon grape should be avoided by pregnant or breastfeeding women. The roots of Oregon grape are medicinal but toxic to the untrained user.

Edible and Useful Parts

Flowers: Use the flowers for decorating drinks, cakes, or salads.

Berries: The berries can be eaten raw and have a sweet though somewhat bitter taste. They can also be cooked and made into jellies or dried to use on top of cereals or in a trail mix.

Other uses: The roots and bark can be made into yellow dye.

Benefits: Oregon grape is well known among herbalists for its medicinal uses.

Sustainability: Oregon grape is fairly common. It is a nice native plant that tolerates shade; you might like to plant it in your High Sierra landscape.

Oregon Grape Jellies

These jellies are kid favorites and not only yummy but also good for slightly upset tummies and to ward off colds. They are also good for adults and can even be served as a fun dessert. You can also use this recipe with elderberries or rose hips.

Ingredients
- 3 cups Oregon grapes
- 1 cup water
- ½ lemon
- 2 cups sugar
- Organic gelatin or vegan alternative—follow package instructions for how much to use

Bring Oregon grapes and water to a quick boil. Mush the berries thoroughly and strain. Place back in the pot and add lemon and sugar. Whisk in the gelatin. Pour into fun molds or a square pan. Let cool in the fridge for a few hours or until fully gelled. Cut into bite-size pieces. Coat with sugar if desired.

PINEAPPLE WEED

Matricaria discoidea
Asteraceae (Other common edible species in this family—daisies,
   artichokes, dandelions, thistles, sunflowers)
Originates in the Pacific Northwest and Asia

—

Pineapple weed is a common weed that grows in disturbed places. You would never guess from its humble appearance that it really does smell like pineapple. Although the Sierra is a beautiful natural region, there are also many areas that are suburban, and pineapple weed thrives there in disturbed places and on roadsides. I don't often use it in cooking, but I like to rub its leaves between my hands so that they smell like pineapple, or put a sprig of it in my water bottle for some fun flavor. It is common all around the world, and recognizing it on travels is a thrill.

Identification: Pineapple weed looks like a mini chamomile plant without as many flower petals. It has a soft green stem with needle-like, feathery leaves and a small nub of a flower that mostly appears as a pineapple-like yellow center, sometimes with a few small white petals. It is very low growing, rarely reaching ten inches. The flowers smell like pineapple when crushed.

Where to Find: You can find pineapple weed in disturbed places, compacted soils, and sidewalk cracks—and near civilization in general.

When to Harvest: Harvest pineapple weed in spring and summer.

How to Harvest: Pinch off just the top part of the plant so that it can produce more flowers, or take the flower.

Poisonous Look-Alikes: There are none that I know of, and especially none that smell like pineapple.

Edible and Useful Parts

Leaves: These can be a bit bitter, but can be added to a salad.

Flowers: You can eat these fresh in a salad or nibble on them while hiking. They can be dried for tea or even ground into a flour. They can also be a nice addition to drinks or used as a fun fragrance in bath products or flavoring in desserts.

Benefits: Like its cousin chamomile, pineapple weed has soothing and relaxing properties.

Sustainability: Pineapple weed is very common.

Pineapple Weed Colada Smoothie

nonalcoholic version

Why not use pineapple weed for novelty in your next piña colada?

Ingredients
- 5 tablespoons pineapple weed tops
- ½ cup water or ice
- 2 fresh or frozen mangoes, peeled and cut
- 1½ cups coconut milk or fresh young coconut
- ½ cup yogurt (or, for a vegan recipe, just add more coconut milk)
- Pinch of salt
- Honey to taste

Blend all ingredients in a blender and enjoy.

PINES AND FIRS

Pinus spp. and *Abies* spp.
Pinaceae
Originate worldwide
—

Fir and pine needles are emblems of Sierra foraging for me. There's nothing quite like taking a snowy bite of fir needles on a winter ski tour or snowshoe hike in the Sierra. I bite down on the icy needles shining in the sun, and the lemony-fresh, slightly bitter taste enlivens my taste buds. I am transformed into a deer or other forest creature for just a moment of being fully attuned to my surroundings. My little daughter loves doing this as well. Pines and firs, which can be used fairly interchangeably, are generous edible trees that you can count on finding pretty much anywhere in the world. I have nibbled on them from the forests of Finland to the mountains of the Himalayas. I love that the most common trees in these mountains are wonderfully edible. I prefer the taste and texture of firs to pines: the short needles are more palatable. Pine trees also produce a crop of delicious pine nuts every year. All of them are edible, but some are much larger than others and therefore more rewarding to harvest.

Identification: Several varieties of pines and firs occur in the Sierra. All are large coniferous evergreen trees with dark-green needles. They produce cones of varying sizes. See the essay following this account for more in-depth identification notes.

Where to Find: Look for pines and firs in forested areas.

When to Harvest: You can harvest parts of these trees any time of year. Nuts are ripe in the fall. Pollen appears in spring or early summer.

How to Harvest: To taste the needles, just bite or pinch them off. Harvesting pine nuts, by contrast, is an art. What I like to do is harvest the cones off the ground when they are still closed. You have to be faster than a squirrel to do this, so it's not always easy. I suggest starting to scope out your local trees in late August and early September. You will also want to bring gloves, as the cones are often sappy, and pine sap is like superglue. Harvest the closed but not green cones off the ground or from the tree and bring them home to dry on a big blanket or tarp. (The tarp or blanket may get sappy, so don't be too attached to it for other purposes.) Let them dry for about three weeks, at which point it should be fairly easy to just shake out the nuts. Before eating any of them, you will want to put the nuts in a bucket of water first: the ones that float are no good, and you should discard those or use the shells to make beads. Even after doing this, you might find that some are bad upon cracking.

Poisonous Look-Alikes: There are none found commonly in the High Sierra. If it smells like a Christmas tree, you're good to go.

Edible and Useful Parts

Needles: The best needles are the teeny young lime-green sprigs that show up in the early summer. The younger the needles, the more tender and less bitter. Older needles can be eaten as well, though; just spit out the unchewable part. They can be eaten raw or cooked. They make a very nice healthy tea or flavoring for drinks, and are an exciting addition to a salad.

Pine nuts: These can be nibbled on as a trail snack and used in many dishes, such as pesto and pastas. To eat them, simply crack the shell and eat the yummy inside. You can freeze pine nuts in their shell. They do go rancid quite fast otherwise, as commercial nuts often do. Nothing beats a freshly harvested pine nut. They are delicious and heart healthy, and many people who cannot eat other nuts can eat them. To harvest tasty nuts that are sufficiently large, you will want to find a pinyon pine. There is only one species in the High Sierra, which is called a one-leaf pinyon pine, and it is only barely in the range covered in this book, as it usually doesn't grow above 5,500 feet. However, I have also harvested the nuts of sugar pines from their giant long cones and even Jeffrey and ponderosa pines with some success. Just know that High Sierra pine nuts are not as reliably abundant as those in the foothills.

Pollen: This is a very abundant and healthy food that is often overlooked. The male cones get covered in pollen in the early spring or summer. Simply shake the cones into a bag. The pollen is so abundant in some seasons that everything gets covered in yellow. In those seasons, you can collect it from any clean surface or just stick your tongue out in the wind. You can sprinkle pollen on cereals, mix it into smoothies, or bake it into baked goods. The entire male cone can also be cooked and eaten. Pine pollen allergies are not common, as the particles are quite large.

Inner bark: The inner bark of pines and firs is a well-known survival food. Harvesting this kills the tree, however, and is only recommended in a survival situation or if forest thinning is needed or a tree needs to be removed.

Other uses: The wood of these trees is obviously useful for a variety of purposes. Pine sap can be made into a superglue by heating it. It has also been used medicinally. The roots can be used for basketry.

Benefits: Pine and fir needles are very high in vitamin C. Pine nuts are high in iron, magnesium, zinc, and protein. They also may lower bad cholesterol. Pine pollen is reported to help testosterone levels in males.

Sustainability: Pines and firs are very common in the High Sierra, and the squirrels will usually hold their own, so you don't have to worry about outcompeting wildlife in this case.

Leave-No-Trace Sierra Sun Tea

There are so many recipes for pines and firs that it was hard to choose just one. This is my favorite, as it can be made on a Sierra backcountry trip and does not harm the tree in any manner.

What you will need:
- Clear plastic bag
- Rubber band
- Pine or fir tree with a low-hanging branch
- Water
- Sun
- Half a day

Find a low-hanging pine or fir branch. Fill a clean plastic bag with water. Put the pine or fir branch in it, and use a rubber band or string to tie the bag to the branch. No need to cut the branch; just tie the bag. Leave it in there for half a day and go about your adventures. Come back to a freshly made and healthy sun tea. Just remove the bag from the branch, thank the branch, and pour your pine- or fir-flavored beverage into a cup, perhaps with some honey. The success of this recipe will depend on how sunny it is and how long you leave the bag.

Identifying High Sierra Pines and Firs

One of the most common questions I am asked by people who are just getting interested in learning more about the species in the Sierra is "What type of tree is this?" This question makes sense, of course, as these amazing tall beings really create the mountain landscape. I encourage people to get to know the trees, to notice what color they are, the texture of their bark, the shape and size of their cones and needles, and even their smell and taste. Just knowing the name of a tree species doesn't really tell you much about the tree. It's better to become familiar with the tree and always recognize its type because you truly know it, even if you call it "the puzzle bark tree" or whatever name you made up for it. It's a bit like going to a party where you don't know anyone. If you go around to all the people at the party and just find out their names but don't really get to know anything about them, you will probably leave the party without having made a single friend—you might not even recognize anyone from the party when you see them at the next event. The following is helpful identification information about the pine and fir trees that grow in the High Sierra, but these facts are just the beginning—there's much more to learn.

There are nine common types of pines, two true firs and one fake fir (the Douglas fir), and one mountain hemlock. Here is a quick method for telling the difference between pines and the other trees:

Do the clap test. Clap your hands gently around the needles of the tree. Can you twirl the needles along your palm with ease because they are needlelike and round, growing in a cluster? Or are they best kept still and flat in your hand because they are flat and growing individually along the branch? If they are round, and usually long, you have just met a pine tree. If they are flat, and usually short, continue on.

Do the cones hang on the branches, or do they grow upright? If they grow upright, you are looking at a true fir. If they hang, continue on.

Are the branches smooth, or do they have little stubs?
Do the cones have little tails hanging out of them as if a small wooden mouse got stuck in there (a story I like to tell)? If they are smooth and the cones have little tails sticking out of each scale, you are in the presence of a Douglas fir. If not, then it's a mountain hemlock.

Another easy way to tell the difference between pines and firs is that firs are the ones that look like Christmas trees—because they are the most common commercial Christmas tree in our area.

White fir

Jeffrey pine

Douglas fir

Mountain hemlock

PLANTAINS

Plantago spp.

Plantaginaceae (Other common edible species in this family—
American brooklime/American speedwell)
Originate in Europe, North America, and northern and central Asia

---

If you were going to an unknown land, which plants would you pack with you? I would probably choose plantain as one of them, and so it seems did the European settlers who came to the Americas. Plantain is sometimes called white man's footsteps, as this useful plant spread with the settlers. It now grows in most places in the United States and is often considered a weed. It has a myriad of medicinal uses, which might explain why Europeans decided to bring it on their long journeys. Although its leaves don't have the most pleasant flavor, its seeds are very good for you and have a nice soft nutty taste. They are commonly known in the supplement aisle as psyllium and are very rich in fiber. By the way, the plantain plant is not at all related to the banana-like plantain (*Musa* x *paradisiaca*), despite the shared common name.

Identification: Plantains are low-growing perennial or annual plants with basal leaves. Plantain leaves are large and oval and have very clear and prominent linear veins on the underside. The flower stalk is slender and long, and forms a bobblehead flower at the top. It has teeny-tiny greenish-white flowers that quickly turn brown. There are three species of plantain in the High Sierra: common plantain (*P. major*), narrow-leaf plantain (*P. lanceolata*), and California plantain (*P. erecta*). They are all interchangeable for our purposes, though California plantain can be a bit hairier, has much smaller leaves, and is therefore less desirable as an edible.

Where to Find: You can find plantains in disturbed places, near human habitation, and in sunny areas.

When to Harvest: These plants can be harvested spring through fall.

How to Harvest: Pinch off the leaves or rub the seeds off the bobblehead seed stalk.

Poisonous Look-Alikes: There are none that I know of with this size of leaf and the clear veins, but if you're in doubt, wait until the flower forms.

Edible and Useful Parts

Leaves: These can be eaten fresh or cooked. You can put the leaves in smoothies and soups. The flavor can be quite bitter, however, so you may want to use the leaves only in small amounts.

Seeds: The seeds can be roasted or eaten fresh. You can sprinkle them on cereals, salads, or smoothies or use them in baking. They are easy to collect by just rubbing them off the seedpod; they do not need to be dehusked.

Benefits: Plantains are high in calcium, minerals, and vitamin A. The leaves are commonly used in salves and poultices to fight infection and treat insect bites; they also can be used internally to help with stomach ulcers. They are my go-to for slightly infected cuts.

Sustainability: Plantains are considered invasive weeds and are very common. California plantain is native, though quite common, but the other two varieties are more desirable for harvesting, so you can let the California plantain be.

Plantain Pudding

Plantain seeds have the awesome property of thickening soups, puddings, and baked goods. They are great for you and can be used in gluten-free or keto-friendly baking.

Ingredients
- 2 cups milk or dairy-free milk
- 6 tablespoons ground plantain seeds
- 3 tablespoons sweetener of your choice
- 1 teaspoon vanilla
- 1 cup berries, raisins, or fruit such as orange or apples

Blend all ingredients in a blender. Pour into containers of your choice and let set in the refrigerator for about an hour. Eat for breakfast or dessert.

PURSLANE

Portulaca oleracea
Portulacaceae (Other common edible species in this family—
  purslane, succulents)
Originates in North Africa, the Middle East, and the Indian subcontinent

———

Purslane is one of the tastiest wild edibles, in my opinion. I love its fresh tart taste and crunchy texture. Purslane is not really very wild; it's mostly a garden weed that travels with nursery transplants by accident. It's not on record as being in the High Sierra, but I have found it many times, growing in piles of soil and in landscaping. Purslane is a common food ingredient in the Middle East. *Portulaca* means "gate" in Latin and *oleracea* means "kitchen vegetable."

Identification: Purslane is a succulent annual plant that often grows along the ground, but can be up to ten inches high. It has oval rounded leaves that are thick, leathery, and numerous. The stems are slightly purple, and the leaves can be as well. Its flowers are bright yellow.

Where to Find: You can find purslane in disturbed places and by human habitation.

When to Harvest: Harvest this plant in summer.

How to Harvest: Just pinch or cut off a leaf, flower, or seed.

Poisonous Look-Alikes: Some spurges look similar, but purslane is succulent and not hairy.

Edible and Useful Parts

Leaves: You can eat the leaves cooked or raw. They are very good in salads or just by themselves as a garnish. They have a slightly acidic taste because they contain oxalic acid. Purslane leaves can be fried, pickled, or steamed. Purslane turns slimy if you cook it too much, but that trait can be nice in a soup or stew.

Flowers: The flowers can be eaten along with the stem and leaves or used as decoration.

Seeds: You can grind the seeds to use as a spice.

Stems: These can be eaten raw or cooked.

Benefits: Purslane is high in vitamins C and A, omega-3s, calcium, magnesium, and potassium.

Sustainability: Purslane is a common, widespread edible.

Persian Purslane Salad

Purslane is usually ready to eat at the hottest time of year, and I find this recipe of tangy purslane and cucumbers very refreshing in the heat.

Ingredients
- 1 European cucumber or several Persian cucumbers
- 2½ cups purslane
- 1 small purple onion
- 1½ cups cherry tomatoes
- ¼ cup chopped mint
- ½ cup olive oil
- Juice of 1 lemon
- Cubes of feta cheese (optional)
- Salt and pepper to taste

Wash and cut up all vegetables. Toss with olive oil, lemon juice, salt, and pepper. Serve with feta cheese and lavash bread or a rice pilaf.

What Is a Weed?

A weed is defined as an unwanted plant or a plant in the wrong place. I've often wondered why we call very useful plants the derogatory term *weed* just because they're robust and resilient. Is a dandelion "a plant in the wrong place" if it happens to grow conveniently in my backyard where I can eat it? Is a nettle "a plant in the wrong place" in someone's flower garden just because the person wants only roses, even if nettles grew there first? If a plant didn't grow in California five hundred years ago, but does now, then is it in the wrong place? Is it an invasive weed? What if it appeared two thousand years ago? Ten thousand?

I certainly respect how difficult it is when a particularly prolific plant takes over other plants' habitat. I have volunteered on land restoration crews many times for that reason and have also had Bermuda grass in my vegetable garden, which anyone who has had that problem knows is precisely that—a problem. Having been an ecologically minded gardener for many years, I also eventually realized that some of this "war against weeds" is really human tyranny over nature, an expression of our wish to have things exactly how we want them instead of how nature is designing them, akin in a small way to such outrageous actions as moving entire rivers and creeks for our convenience. People even take to blasting tiny plants with toxins like Roundup, which poison children and our waterways, just to have a perfect lawn where there never was a lawn before. That seems extreme to me and ultimately more of a war we're waging against ourselves.

Many of the plants in this book fall into the weed category, and thank goodness they do, as it means they are widely available and that there is no concern about overharvesting. So yes, let's fiercely preserve and protect native plant habitat so that we benefit from an intact, healthy ecosystem, but let's not forget that the weeds are not simply waste plants to be pulled and killed. These common and widely spread plants, which have managed to do well despite human-induced changes and have so many gifts to give, deserve to be appreciated and ennobled, not just called weeds.

Perhaps instead of fighting against so-called weeds in a garden, we should actually just give in and make a superfood weed garden. This would also be the more ecological approach, as it would avoid our having to bring in a ton of fertilizer, soil, and other inputs to grow a tomato that's really no less a weed than dock. There is definitely wisdom in choosing to grow only those plants that naturally thrive in a place, rather than making gardening an unnatural effort. Were we to cultivate and learn to include more plants in our diet that grow in our landscape with ease, we could reduce unnatural inputs and water usage in our gardens.

That being said, sometimes removing some thistles or blackberry is exactly what is needed to create space for a healthier habitat. This is where we humans get to exercise our great gift of being mindful caretakers. Ideally we observe and listen to the landscape, not being attached to our own ideas but noting what would best serve that ecosystem and then trying to act on that understanding. Perhaps a controlled burn is needed? Perhaps certain plants need to be removed, and other existing plants tended? Of course, this is not always easy to do, but at least if we take the step of observing and listening and remembering that sometimes the weeds are the gift, we might make better, more ecologically whole choices.

Give the weeds a chance. Or just eat them.

ROSES

Rosa spp.

Rosaceae (Other common edible species in this family—apples, strawberries, raspberries)

Originate in various places, including North America

———

Roses are actually one of the most abundant and delicious wild edibles in the Sierra. These thorny shrubs with their beautiful pink flowers and delicious berries called rose hips grow all over the place near where I live in the Tahoe area. They also grew all over the place where I was a child in Finland, but were much bigger. My daughter and I eat rose hips all season, late into the fall and even sometimes in the winter as they peek out of the snow before they rot. She likes to eat the whole thing and doesn't mind the seeds; I nibble the outside and toss the seeds. So many people don't know that these delicious and easy-to-identify tiny fruit are all around them. There are three main types of roses in the High Sierra: California rose (*R. californica*), wood rose (*R. gymnocarpa*), and pine rose (*R. pinetorum*). There are also planted roses, of course. All are edible, as long as they have not been treated with chemicals. The only difficulty with rose hips is that they contain numerous white seeds that can sometimes be a bit hairy and itchy in your mouth. In fact, as kids we used to use them as itching powder and throw them on each other. So when using the fruit, you would usually want to discard the seeds unless you are somehow able to eat them the way that my squirrel of a daughter can.

Identification: Sierra roses are thorny shrubs up to five feet tall. They have pinnately divided leaflets, meaning that their leaves grow in formations of three to eleven leaflets per leaf. The leaves are green to purplish, turning beautiful colors in the fall. The stems are usually very thorny. The fruit of the rose, rose hips, are small and oval, and orange-red when ripe. Each rose hip has a little brown multipart tail at the end, which makes them easy to identify.

Where to Find: Roses can be found in partially shady areas, open spots in woods, suburban areas, and in the understory of coniferous forests.

When to Harvest: Harvest these plants from spring to early winter.

How to Harvest: Simply pick off the desired part.

Poisonous Look-Alikes: There are none that I can think of with this many thorns.

Edible and Useful Parts

Flowers: Beautiful rose flowers can be dried and used for flavoring, delicious tea, or even a bath. They can also be used for decoration on dishes. Rose water can be made by putting fresh petals in a jar with a spoonful of strong alcohol, such as vodka. Shake the jar vigorously to allow the essence of the roses to escape into the alcohol. Let the alcohol evaporate out. Then add just enough water to cover the petals. Let soak for twenty-four hours. Strain out the petals. Keep in the fridge and use as a spritzer or flavoring.

Rose hips: The tangy but sweet taste of rose hips is delicious. They can be cooked into jams, jelly, drinks, and soup. They can also be dried and used for tea or powdered for use as a superfood in smoothies and cereals. They can also be eaten fresh off the bush. The least labor-intensive way to remove the seeds is to cook the hips with a bit of water and then strain the seeds out. This pulp can then be dehydrated and powdered, or used in recipes fresh. Otherwise you have to open each one and manually remove the seeds, which is a lot of effort.

Benefits: Rose hips are very high in vitamins C and A.

Sustainability: Roses are very common.

Rose Hip Smoothie

This superfood smoothie is a delicious breakfast before a good day out.

Ingredients
- 3 cups of rose hips, washed
- 1 banana
- Handful of frozen raspberries
- Handful of frozen peaches
- A bit of honey if desired

Prepare rose hip mush in advance. It can be refrigerated for about a week or frozen for much longer. To make mush: Add the rose hips to a big pot, then barely cover the rose hips with water. Boil for at least 30 minutes until it's easy to separate the seeds from the fruit by mushing them. Blend the mixture on low until fully mixed. Strain the seeds out with a strainer. Blend a cup of this mush with the other smoothie ingredients. Enjoy.

SAGEBRUSH

Artemisia tridentata and other species
Asteraceae (Other common edible species in this family—daisies,
 artichokes, dandelions, thistles, sunflowers)
Originate in the North American West

————

Sagebrush, which defines many parts of the high-desert landscape, is an essential flavor in a Sierra stew. When I'm not in the mountains, I miss the smell of fresh sagebrush on a high-desert hike. It's one of those smells that sparks memories, much as Jeffrey pines do on a hot day, and it embodies the smell of home for me. I often just rub my hands gently along a sagebrush twig to capture the smell. Sometimes I break off a little piece and rub some on my neck or ankles or wrists for an instant refreshing and cleansing moment and to help repel insects as well. The words *sage* and *sagebrush* are often used interchangeably, and the two types of plants are interchangeable in their uses and scent, but despite their similarities, they are completely different plants. Sage (*Salvia* spp.) has large, soft, oval leaves often covered in a bit of hair. Sagebrush (*Artemisia* spp.) is the woody-stemmed plant we see all over the High Sierra, with tiny light-green leaves. There are nine types of sagebrush and one type of sage (*Salvia pachyphylla*) commonly found in the High Sierra. Everything said here about using sagebrush also applies to sage, except that the sage is much more rare.

Identification: Sagebrush is a common woody shrub one to six feet tall, with small pale grayish green foliage. The leaves have little lobes at the tips. The flowers are small and yellow. The plant is very aromatic.

Where to Find: Sagebrush grows in dry places in full sun.

When to Harvest: You can harvest this plant in spring, summer, and fall.

How to Harvest: Cut or pinch off a sprig; collect seeds in a bag.

Poisonous Look-Alikes: There are none that I know of that smell like sagebrush.

Caution: All members of the *Artemisia* genus can be toxic if consumed in large amounts.

Edible and Useful Parts

Leaves: Either cooked or raw, the richly aromatic leaves of sagebrush can be used in small amounts to flavor dishes and teas. They go well in a stew or with meats. They are also useful in food preservation, as they are antimicrobial. They can also be used in cleaning products, shampoos, and deodorants, and as a smudge.

Flowers: You can use these for decoration or as a spice fresh or dried.

Seeds: The dry seeds can be ground into an aromatic flour.

Other uses: The wood is highly flammable and can be used in fire making. As mentioned earlier, the whole plant is antibacterial and antimicrobial, and has multiple medicinal uses.

Benefits: Sagebrush is considered a highly purifying medicinal plant.

Sustainability: Sagebrush is very common in the High Sierra.

Slow-Cooked Sagebrush Chicken

This is a great meal to prepare before heading outdoors in the Sierra for a full day. It takes 15 minutes to get it started in the morning and is ready to go when you come home hungry.

Ingredients
- 1 whole chicken
- 1 onion
- 4 sprigs sagebrush
- Salt and pepper

Cut the onion into pieces and place in a slow cooker. Prepare the chicken. Make sure the giblets have been removed. Rub the chicken with salt, pepper, and one of the sagebrush sprigs. Place the sagebrush sprigs and salt and pepper in the cavity. Place the chicken in the slow cooker and cook for 7–8 hours. Remove the chicken carefully, as it will be very hot. Serve with your favorite sides.

SALSIFY

Tragopogon dubius and related species
Asteraceae (Other common edible species in this family—daisies,
  artichokes, dandelions, thistles, sunflowers)
Originate in Eurasia and western Africa

———

I first met salsify as a garden weed in a school garden where I used to work.
It was the purple variety. I had noticed it already the first year I worked there
because of its showy, puffy seed balls that look like giant dandelions. I did a
bit of research and found out that although it was growing outside the garden
beds, it was quite the wild edible superstar. I tasted a piece and determined
that it was delicious. I wondered why it wasn't being grown more and sold in
stores—I'm still wondering that. It is mentioned as a food in European texts
as far back as the thirteenth century and was introduced in California from
southern and central Europe, where it has been cultivated as a food plant
for hundreds of years. Being a well-loved plant, salsify goes by many names,
including goat's beard, wild oyster plant, and Johnny go-to-bed-at-noon.

Salsify has done quite well spreading here in Tahoe, and yellow salsify
plants can be seen blooming just about anywhere in June.

Identification: To me, salsify looks
like a cross between a giant grass and
a beautiful daisy. It has a stalk that's
from seven to twenty-five inches
tall and a brilliant two-to-four-inch
flower that can be yellow or purple. It
grows as an annual or biannual from
a basal rosette of thin leaves. It has
several easy-to-identify features:

Milky sap. Like all its fellow members
in the thistle and dandelion family,
salsify has stems that exude white sap
when you break them. By the way,
the milky sap can get pretty sticky on
fingers and clothes and can even be
slightly irritating to eat, so I suggest
washing it off.

"Wool." If you look at where salsify
touches the ground or where the
leaves split from the stalk, you might
see some cottony fluff there.

Tap root. Salsify has a long tap root,
more like a carrot than a bulb.

Early bedtime. Maybe not a great
identification feature, but a fun
little fact: salsify flowers close in the
afternoon, making them a bit harder
to identify later in the day.

Where to Find: Salsify grows in sunny
meadows, on roadsides, and at sunny
forest edges.

When to Harvest: The ideal time to
harvest salsify is before it goes to
seed in spring and early summer.
Harvesting it once it is in seed is not
ideal for eating and could also cause
the plant to spread invasively.

How to Harvest: Dig up salsify roots
using a trowel, stick, or small shovel.
Cut off the stem with scissors or a

sharp knife. Grow your own salsify in moist soil; you can even collect seeds from a wild plant.

Poisonous Look-Alikes: Some of the poisonous possible look-alikes, such as daffodils, would have a clear bulb. If in doubt, wait until the plant flowers or seeds and then salsify is quite easy to identify.

Edible and Useful Parts

As is true of most of the members of its family, all parts of salsify are edible.

Leaves: The leaves can be eaten as a salad green or cooked; young leaves are best.

Flowers: The unopened flower heads are delicious eaten raw; the flower can be eaten at any stage.

Stalks: The stalk is usually too tough to eat, but you can use it to make a broth.

Roots: Dig up and use as a root vegetable, or eat it raw, as you would a carrot. It's best before the plant is fully flowering. The root is usually too tough once the plant has gone to seed. The purple variety's root is large and quite delicious; some say it has an oyster-like taste. The yellow variety can be a bit smaller and tastes more like asparagus than oysters. There's no need to peel the root; just wash it well.

The roots of the wild yellow salsify that grows in dry mountain meadows can be quite tough. One reason why salsify may have lost popularity as a root vegetable is that it doesn't preserve very well. The roots tend to wilt quickly, so harvest them right before you are ready to eat them. It's good to use a trowel or small shovel to harvest so that you get the whole root.

Benefits: Salsify is a superfood. It's rich in potassium, iron, vitamin C, thiamin, calcium, and phosphorous.

Sustainability: Often an introduced species, it's fine to harvest salsify in places where it's abundant.

Simple Salsify Stir-Fry

Stir-fries are an easy way to incorporate wild foods. In this recipe salsify stalks are similar to asparagus or bamboo shoots. Just make sure you have soft, young salsify roots that are well peeled, or they will be too hard to use.

Ingredients
- Handful of salsify roots, well washed, lightly peeled, and cut into pieces
- Salsify leaves
- 4 potatoes, chopped
- 3 tablespoons cooking oil of your choice
- Salt
- Pepper
- Other vegetables if you wish

Wash the salsify roots and potatoes and boil or steam them for 20–30 minutes. Toss them into a pan with the oil and the leaves and season with salt and pepper to taste. You can also add any other vegetables of your choice.

Would You Like to Have Your Picture Taken?
The Photo Personalities of Plants

Part of writing this book was taking pictures of plants in all seasons.
I did the same in 2011 for my first book, *The Bay Area Forager*, and
had already noticed then that some plants seemed to be photogenic
while others, much to my chagrin, just did not want their picture taken.
Salsify was one of those. The flower was easy to capture, but the tall,
slender stalk just drowned into the background and didn't seem to
fit on the screen. Its cousin dandelion, by contrast, loves to be photo-
graphed. I think I have more than fifty pictures of dandelion in different
environments. It seems to just scream out, "Here I am—notice me!" and
the photos turn out great. Violets and hazelnuts also tend to be shy;
dock is readily available for a straightforward portrait. Perhaps you're
thinking, "Well, Mia, that's a cute idea, but it's really just lighting and
shapes," and you might be right, but the more I work with plants, the
more I have come to see them as having personalities with different
traits. In fact, on my wild food walks, I tend to tell people that I will introduce them to some of my friends—meaning the plants—and I often
get quite excited to notice a "friend" I haven't seen in a while. Perhaps
that's what really getting to know a landscape does.

Salsify

Dandelion

Dock

Shy violet

SERVICEBERRIES

Amelanchier spp.

Rosaceae (Other common edible species in this family—roses, apples, strawberries, raspberries)

Originate in North America

When Sierra meadows bloom with serviceberries in the late spring, the white flowers are so profuse that it's as if the snow has fallen again. These berries are so abundant that I was surprised when I first found out they were edible. They are related to medlars, a more rare, almost apple-like fruit that used to be more popular in earlier times in Europe. The scientific name *Amelanchier* is French and means "medlar." The serviceberries I have sampled have been quite plain, unlike sweet medlars—edible but not necessarily flavorful. I have heard that they can be more juicy and sweet in other places, however, and I have seen pictures of serviceberries that look moist like grapes. Maybe the ones I have gathered have grown in drier areas, as they have been mealy. The fruit is ripe when purple, not red, and is ready in the summer. There are two types of serviceberries in the High Sierra: alder-leaf serviceberry (*A. alnifolia*) and Utah serviceberry (*A. utahensis*). Both are edible.

Identification: Serviceberries are woody shrubs or small trees up to ten feet tall. They have small oval leaves that are serrated toward the end. True to the Rosaceae family, their small flowers are white with five petals, and there are many of them on the plant. Those are followed by the small edible berries that turn red at first and then purple.

Where to Find: Depending on the variety, this plant can be found in meadows, moist places, and dry rocky slopes.

When to Harvest: Harvest serviceberries in summer.

How to Harvest: Pick the berries when they are purple.

Poisonous Look-Alikes: There are none that I know of that are common to the High Sierra.

Caution: Like most stone-fruit seeds, serviceberry seeds contain small amounts of cyanide, which is destroyed by cooking.

Edible and Useful Parts

Berries: You can eat them fresh or cooked. Serviceberries can be made into jellies or used with apples or other fruit in recipes. They can also be dried and put into baked goods or cereals. The berries can also be made into a purple dye.

Benefits: Serviceberries have medicinal benefits. They are high in vitamin B2 and many minerals.

Sustainability: Serviceberries tend to be abundant.

Serviceberry Pemmican

Pemmican is a great trail snack. It stores well, is very portable, and has high fat content, which is good for sustained outdoor exploration. It contains good ol'-fashioned protein and fat, unlike some sugary trail bar. It is traditionally made with bison meat and fat by Native Americans, but you can use another type of red game meat.

Ingredients
- 4 cups meat, double ground
- 1 cup serviceberries
- 1 cup currants or other wild or nonwild dried berries
- 1 cup wild or store-bought nuts or seeds of your choice
- 3 cups tallow (heated meat fat)
- Salt and pepper to taste

Dry the meat overnight in a dehydrator or at 150° in an oven. Powder it as much as possible in a blender or food processor. Mix all ingredients together. Spread onto a baking sheet. Let cool and cut into strips. Enjoy on your next adventure.

Are All Berries Edible?

Whether all berries are edible is a question I get asked often. Unfortunately, they aren't. Some are delicious, some don't taste that good, some aren't pleasant, and others are poisonous. As I mentioned earlier, some common myths are that all red berries are poisonous or that you can watch animals to see which berries to eat. Neither is true in all cases. There are many delicious red berries, and some animals can eat plants that humans can't. There are a couple common berries in the Sierra that are not really poisonous but shouldn't be eaten, such as the white snowberries you will see everywhere in the summer. There is a berry in the Midwest that also goes by the name of snowberry and looks about the same; it is edible, but the one in the Sierra is not. Then there are also mealy serviceberries, mentioned earlier, that are edible but not the most delicious. There isn't really a blanket rule for determining which berries are edible, so it's best to get to know them individually.

SIERRA GOOSEBERRY

Ribes roezlii and related species
Grossulariaceae (Other common edible species in this family—currants)
Originates in the western United States

This little hedgehog of a berry sure has thorns, so it must be protecting something really tasty. Sierra gooseberries look like little balls of red spines. I was lucky enough to grow up with only slightly hairy gooseberries, but, loving their flavor, I knew I had to taste this one too despite its hefty protection mechanism. They are delicious, but removing the spikes can be difficult, which limits your options. That's for the best, as they are a rare native berry. There are several species in the High Sierra, some of which are not as spiky; they and all of their relatives in the currant family are edible, though some don't taste as good as others.

Identification: Gooseberries are shrubs up to six feet tall and wide. They have almost maple-like leaves that can turn reddish as they age. The flowers of gooseberries are often very beautiful, white and dark red, hanging from the plant like shooting stars. The berries are distinct, dark red or purple with spikes of the same color. The stems of gooseberries are covered in small thorns.

Where to Find: You can find gooseberries in openings in wooded areas near creeks and rivers.

When to Harvest: Harvest this plant in summer.

How to Harvest: You may want to use gloves to remove the berries, though I find that the thorns are actually fairly soft to the touch.

Poisonous Look-Alikes: There are none to my knowledge.

Edible and Useful Parts

Leaves: Fresh or dried leaves can be used in tea or even as wrapping "paper." Eating wilted leaves is not recommended, as they could be toxic.

Flowers: Flowers can be eaten as a trail treat, used as a decoration, or dried for tea.

Berries: The berries can be eaten fresh or cooked. You can just peel the spikes off on the trail and eat the sweet inside. Some people burn off the spikes, but I find that difficult to do. The easiest way to use the berries is to squish them through a sieve and use the juice for drinks, juices, or jam.

Benefits: Gooseberries are high in vitamin C and copper.

Sustainability: These are native shrubs. Harvest sparingly.

Sierra Gooseberry Cordial

This is a lovely-colored summer refresher.

Ingredients
- Handful of gooseberries
- ½ cup of your choice of sweetener (to taste)
- 1 lime or lemon
- ½ cup water, perhaps from a Sierra spring

Crush the gooseberries through a sieve into a small saucepan. Juice the lime or lemon and add it to the pan. Add the sweetener and water, bring to a boil, and remove from heat. Put the mixture in a jar and let stand overnight. Serve with ice and maybe a wild mint leaf.

SPRING BEAUTIES

Claytonia spp.

Montiaceae (Other common edible species in this family—
  miner's lettuce, montia)
Originate in mountain chains of Asia and North America

This tiny pink-and-white-flowered plant is one of the earliest edibles to appear in the spring, hence the name "spring beauty." There are many species of spring beauties, and they are closely related to the commonly eaten miner's lettuce that grows at lower altitudes. Some spring beauties have starchy corms that are the size of a small walnut, which have been aptly nicknamed "fairy spuds." Unfortunately, most of the spring beauties I have found in the Sierra have had teeny-tiny corms or have been hard to dig up without breaking, but I will keep looking.

Identification: Spring beauties are perennial low-growing flowers one to five inches high. The sometimes purplish stem has one or two basal, lance-shaped leaves that are succulent in nature and might be gone by the time the flower appears. The flowers have five pink-streaked white petals. The common species in the High Sierra are truncate-leaved claytonia (*C. cordifolia*), Western spring beauty (*C. lanceolata*), fell fields claytonia (*C. megarhiza*), Sierra claytonia (*C. nevadensis*), marsh claytonia (*C. palustris*), and occasionally miner's lettuce (*C. perfoliata*). Miner's lettuce has larger leaves shaped like an upside-down umbrella and a tiny white or pinkish flower in the middle. All of these *Claytonia* species can be eaten; some, like miner's lettuce, don't have much of a corm at all, but the leaves are still delicious.

Where to Find: Spring beauties grow in meadows, near melting snow, and in woodlands; they prefer partial shade.

When to Harvest: Harvest these plants in spring.

How to Harvest: Pinch off a leaf or dig up the corm very carefully.

Poisonous Look-Alikes: The leaves of many plants when young could resemble spring beauty leaves, including death camas, so wait until the plant flowers if you're not sure. A key identification clue is that leaves of the *Claytonia* genus are succulent in nature.

Edible and Useful Parts

Leaves: You can eat the leaves raw or cooked in salads or as a green.

Flowers: Eat the flowers raw in salads or use them as decoration.

Corms: These can be eaten raw or cooked, though they are better cooked. Treat them like a mini potato. They taste a bit sweeter than potatoes. The corms are best harvested before the plant flowers. They need to be peeled before cooking, which can be a lot of work.

Benefits: *Claytonia* species are high in vitamins A and C.

Sustainability: Spring beauties can either be very rare or abundant. They take a long time to grow and establish, so I don't recommend harvesting any in places where they are not clearly abundant. Miner's lettuce is often very abundant, and harvesting it should not be of concern.

Sierra Spring Salad

Many wild greens are delicious eaten fresh right after collecting. Salads with wild greens are much heftier than ones with cultivated greens, so do not exect to be able to eat as big a portion. I like blending the wild greens with cultivated ones for that reason.

Ingredients
- Miner's lettuce
- Spring beauty (if abundant)
- Young fireweed leaves
- A few young yarrow sprigs
- Other store-bought or homegrown salad mix of your choice

Dressing:
- Olive oil
- Lemon
- 1 teaspoon honey
- Fresh fir needles cut up very small
- A bit of salt and pepper

Wash all greens carefully. Shake up dressing in a jar. Garnish with edible flowers.

STINGING NETTLE

Urtica dioica
Urticaceae (Other common edible species in this family—baby's tears, clearweed)
Originates in Europe, Asia, and Africa

Stinging nettle is one of my favorite plants to forage. It's one of the only plants that I harvest in quantity each year. I often even freeze it or dry it for future use. This endorsement means a lot coming from me, since I'm more of a deer-style forager, harvesting just bits and pieces of edible plants as I see them. I don't usually harvest large quantities to take home and cook. Stinging nettle is an exception for good reason.

To start with, stinging nettle has a myriad of health benefits, including being a great herb for alleviating allergies. A mineral-rich superfood, stinging nettle is high in calcium, iron, magnesium, and vitamins K, A, and B6. Not only is this plant edible and medicinal—it can also be used for fiber; I even have a shirt made out of stinging nettle! I drink stinging nettle tea almost every day because it keeps my seasonal allergies in check, and I feel as though including this superfood in my diet regularly makes me a superstar too.

By now you're probably wanting to know where and how you can find this amazing plant. So let's get on with it.

Identification: Stinging nettle grows two to five feet tall and has opposite-branching sawtoothed oblong leaves. If you look closely, you can see little hairs on the leaves. Watch out: they sting. The leaves are heavily veined on the underside. The stem is square and covered in hairy stingers as well. Stinging nettle has a distinctive powerful green smell that you can identify by crushing a leaf once you get to know it. One way to be sure you've found it is to let it sting you. Or you can wait until it flowers, though then it's too late to harvest. Stinging nettle flowers are greenish white and quite nondescript; look-alike plants, such as mints, vervains and hedge-nettle, have much more colorful, showy flowers.

Where to Find: Look for nettle near creeks and waterways, in the shade.

When to Harvest: Harvest nettles in spring and summer before they flower.

How to Harvest: If you harvest nettle the right way, it will grow back at least once or twice, so it's very worthwhile learning how. Just cut the stalk with scissors or a knife about a quarter-inch above any pair of leaves toward the top of the plant, usually two or three leaf pairs down. If you don't want to get stung, use scissors and/or gloves. You can actually prolong the harvesting season of a nettle plant in this way.

Poisonous Look-Alikes: There are no poisonous ones I know of.

Edible and Useful Parts

Leaves: Nettle can be eaten raw or cooked. The little stingers, which are actually mechanical injectors of formic acid, need to be broken so that they no longer hurt you. Blending, crushing, and mushing all work. Simply cooking the leaf is not enough.

Nettle can be used much like spinach in any dish and has a delicious soft yet green flavor. My favorites are nettle lasagna, nettle pesto, or simply nettle with garlic and butter. It's a very versatile ingredient—someone once even made me nettle tempura. You can also put it in any smoothie. Blending it is an easy way to destroy the stingers.

Another option is to dry the leaves. Just lay them out in a dry place for some days or use a dehydrator. They can then be crushed and used for a very healthy tea, or powdered and used in smoothies or cereals.

Roots: The roots can be used to make tea.

Other uses: The stalks can be made into cordage and fabric.

Benefits: As I've already described, stinging nettle really is a superfood very high in minerals and with multiple health benefits.

Sustainability: Nettle is quite abundant in the Sierra, and many consider it a nuisance, as it is not native. That, along with the fact that it grows back easily if you harvest it the right way, makes it a plant that you can harvest in quantity.

Nettles are also great to grow in a container or in your garden. They prefer partial shade and regular water, though they can become quite drought tolerant.

Mia's Grandma's Nettle Soup

This is a soup I grew up eating during the summers I'd spend at my grandmother's summer cottage. My grandmother usually served it with a lightly cooked egg on top, but that is completely optional. This recipe can easily be made vegan by substituting the cream with a dairy-free milk.

Ingredients
- Approximately 6 heaping cups nettle leaves
- 1 onion
- 1 tablespoon butter or oil
- 3 tablespoons glutenous flour or starch
- 2½ cups broth of your choice
- 1 cup white wine
- 1 cup cream (or nondairy milk)
- Salt and pepper to taste

Note: Some nettles are drier than others and soak up a lot of water. If you notice that being the case, just add some more broth.

Mince the onion and place it in a large pot with butter or oil. Fry until translucent. Add flour and fry, but only lightly. Add broth and nettles and bring to a quick boil. Turn the heat down immediately when it boils so as not to destroy the nutritional value of the nettles. Add wine, cream, salt, and pepper. Stir frequently and don't allow it to boil. Once it is heated through, place it in a blender and blend until smooth. Serve with a lightly cooked sliced egg on top and some dark rye bread for a traditional Finnish meal.

Forager Trick: Impress Your Friends by Harvesting Nettle with Your Bare Hands

Earlier this year, my sweet new neighbors came one by one to tell me that I should "watch out for that awful plant over there" and keep my kids away, as it "hurts a ton." I explained to them one by one that I love nettles and was just about to go harvest some for dinner, that I grew up with them and have fallen in a bush of nettles several times, and that they are great for our health. Most looked at me as though I was a bit cuckoo and left it at that. One day, perhaps not in one of my most humble moments, perhaps wanting to defend my dear nettle from being called a nuisance, or perhaps just not wanting to repeat the same spiel again to the third kind neighbor, I instead replied with, "Oh, you mean stinging nettle? I love stinging nettle" as I walked over to the nettle patch, picked off a leaf, and popped it in my mouth. That neighbor was surprised.

I first learned this trick from my younger brother, who used to run after me with a nettle leaf saying "It doesn't hurt," and though he sometimes touched me with it so that it did hurt, it actually is true that you can harvest nettle with your bare hands without getting stung.

First a bit about the sting of the nettle so that you can see how it works. The stingers of nettles are actually little hollow tubes of silica that inject histamine and serotonin into your skin. This is not dangerous, but it can be painful and irritating and last for several hours. Some people actually believe there are health benefits to getting stung, sort of a natural acupuncture, and sting themselves on purpose. Because the stingers are fragile hollow tubes, simply crushing them will render them painless.

So to harvest nettles without gloves, all you need to do is apply a quick, even pressure to the leaf with thumb and forefinger. This will crush the stingers. Then pull the piece off gently. Fold it carefully into a little pillow so that the underside is on top, and crush it all over. Then just put it into your mouth and chew. This works because most people's fingertips are hardy enough that they don't feel the first sting and can break the tube. If you have particularly sensitive fingertips or a particularly stingy nettle, this tactic may not work for you. Usually when I do this a lot, I do get stung slightly on my fingertips, but it doesn't really bother me, and fresh nettle is really tasty. Also being a bit daring and impressing some friends can be enough fun to make up for a little sting.

STRAWBERRIES

Fragaria vesca and *Fragaria virginiana*
Rosaceae (Other common edible species in this family—roses, apples,
   raspberries)
Originates in North America

___

Although I grew up eating wild strawberries, I have not yet had the luck of
tasting a Sierra strawberry. I see plenty of leaves, but can't seem to catch
the berries in time. Perhaps there are not very many berries, and the animal
inhabitants of the forest get to them way before I do. Of course, you can also
eat the nutritious strawberry leaves, but they are not quite as tasty as the
berries. There is only one naturally occurring type of strawberry in the High
Sierra, broad-petal strawberry.

Identification: Wild strawberries look like cultivated strawberries except smaller. They have serrated leaves usually in leaflets of three, and white flowers with yellow centers.

Where to Find: You can find strawberries growing in partially sunny woods, in moist, rich soil.

When to Harvest: Harvest strawberries in summer.

How to Harvest: You can simply pick the leaf or berry.

Poisonous Look-Alikes: There are none to my knowledge. Cinquefoils look very similar, but are also edible.

Edible and Useful Parts

Leaves: These can be eaten raw or cooked; they're best when young. The leaves can also be made into a tea.

Berries: Enjoy the berries raw or cooked.

Benefits: Strawberries are high in vitamins C and K, potassium, and other minerals.

Sustainability: Wild strawberries should only be sampled, as the animals love them and the fruit is not common.

TARWEEDS

Madia spp.

Asteraceae (Other common edible species in this family—daisies, artichokes, dandelions, thistles, sunflowers)

Originate in the United States and the Americas

I love the sweet, pungent smell of tarweed on a hot summer's day. The plant's tenacious and beautiful yellow flowers cover dry areas that would otherwise be barren of flowers in the summer heat of the Sierra. The flowers look so delicate, but they're very drought hardy and stay in bloom a long time. They grow in more abundance than many other wildflower species, and I wonder whether two hundred years ago, when wildflowers were even more abundant, they would have transformed hot meadows into a dense sea of yellow. There are still enough of them now that collecting the tiny, flavorful edible seeds is a possibility, but more as a sample than as a full meal. The main type of tarweed in the High Sierra is common madia (*M. elegans*). Miniature tarweed (*Hemizonella minima*) and Yosemite tarweed (*M. yosemitana*) can also be found, but these are more rare.

Identification: Tarweed is a low-growing annual plant with slender stems and narrow leaves. Its flowers are small but showy, with bright-yellow petals and sometimes a rusty-red center. The seeds are tiny and black. Tarweeds are so called because they have a sticky substance on their stems and flowers that smells a bit like tar. This is an easy way to identify them.

Where to Find: Tarweed grows in dry sunny meadows and on sunny slopes.

When to Harvest: Harvest tarweed in late summer or early fall.

How to Harvest: Wait until the seeds are fully dry in their pods. Rub them out with your fingers or gently hit the plants with something like a small tennis or badminton racket with a bag underneath to collect the seeds. Because tarweeds are sticky, you may find this difficult.

Poisonous Look-Alikes: Other asters look similar to tarweed and are rarely poisonous, but they might not be edible. Because foraging for the seeds is the goal, notice the plant's stickiness and fragrance when it blooms, and you will be certain it's tarweed, as there is no other similar plant with those properties.

Edible and Useful Parts

Seeds: The fragrant seeds of tarweed can be roasted and sprinkled on salads or baked goods. They can be dried or roasted and then ground into a flour. You can also press them into a rich oil.

Benefits: Tarweed seeds are rich in omega oils and protein.

Sustainability: Tarweed is usually still abundant. Plant it in your garden, as it provides late-season color, and butterflies and other insects love it.

Flower Power Cookies

The seeds of many beautiful flowers provide a protein-, mineral-, and omega-oil-rich food that most of us rarely take advantage of. This recipe uses readily available chia seeds to compensate for the lack of wildflower seed abundance, but if you have edible wildflower seeds from plants that you have grown in your yard, such as tarweed, mint, violets, or borage, you can put them in the mix too. A nice property of flower seeds is that they tend to bind water, which means that recipes don't require eggs.

Ingredients
- ½ cup edible flower seeds, such as tarweed and chia
- 1 cup all-purpose flour
- ¼ cup sugar
- ¾ cup butter, softened
- 1 teaspoon vanilla

Preheat oven to 350°. Lightly roast the seeds by tossing them on a medium-hot pan for just a few seconds. Do not over-roast, or your cookies will have a burnt flavor. Let cool and grind into a flour either by hand with a mortar and pestle (which is a workout) or in a heavier-duty blender or coffee grinder. Mix butter, sugar, and vanilla together in a bowl. Add the flower flour and regular flour. Mix until smooth. Roll into a ball and refrigerate for 30 minutes. On a floured surface, roll the ball into a thin sheet and cut it with cookie cutters—possibly flower shapes? Place them on a greased baking sheet. If you want a quick-and-easy version and don't care about looks, you can skip the refrigeration step and just plop the dough onto a greased baking sheet in small lumps and flatten them out with your fingers. Bake for 10–12 minutes. Let cool and serve, or frost with your favorite frosting and sprinkle some seeds on top.

THIMBLEBERRY

Rubus parviflorus
Rosaceae (Other common edible species in this family—roses, apples, strawberries, raspberries)
Originates in northern temperate regions of North America

Thimbleberries are definitely a contender for the tastiest wild edible of the High Sierra. The bears and other forest animals might agree, as does my family. "Are they ripe yet?" my kids will ask, looking through the thimbleberry leaf forest in a treasure hunt for the little berries. Thimbleberries are aptly named, as they really do look like soft, squishy red thimbles; they are relatives of raspberries and blackberries. I like their wonderful soft flavor even more than the taste of raspberries, but they do not preserve or travel well, which is probably why they have not become more popular in stores.

Identification: Thimbleberries are deciduous shrubs that are about one to four feet tall in this area. They have hand-size fuzzy green leaves that are similar to maple leaves in shape but with softer edges. The flowers are white with yellow centers. The berries are red and raspberry-like, but flatter.

Where to Find: You can find thimbleberries in shadier places, as forest ground cover, and in moist places.

When to Harvest: Harvest thimbleberries in summer.

How to Harvest: You can simply pick the berries.

Poisonous Look-Alikes: There are none that I know of in this area.

Edible and Useful Parts

Leaves: The leaves can be used for tea.

Berries: Wait until the berries are fully red and soft to pick them. They can be eaten raw or cooked in any berry recipe. They make a delicious jam, fruit leather, sorbet, and so much more.

Benefits: Thimbleberries are rich in vitamins A and C, potassium, and iron.

Sustainability: Thimbleberries are a favorite of wildlife, but there are also often plenty of them for humans. Get to know your area to see whether there tend to be a lot.

Thimbleberry Ice Cream Swirl

Here in the High Sierra, thimbleberries are so precious that I rarely cook with them. I know they can be much more prolific elsewhere and that the plants can grow taller than people, but here we just eat them as we pick. And as I mentioned, they don't keep well. Here's a very simple instant-gratification recipe that kids of all ages love or that can get you into a kid-like state of fun ice cream mushing.

Ingredients
- Handful of thimbleberries
- 1 tablespoon honey
- Vanilla ice cream, melted to be a bit softer
- Cookies of your choice

Scoop the softened ice cream into bowls. Plop a handful of thimbleberries on top (if you've managed to save them this long!). Crumble your cookies on top. Dip a spoon into honey. Take the spoon and stir the ice cream and other ingredients. Watch it turn pink. Enjoy.

THISTLES

Cirsium spp.
Asteraceae (Other common edible species in this family—daisies,
   artichokes, dandelions, sunflowers)
Originate in various places

—

Spiky thistles may not appear to be very edible at first, but they are actually
quite delicious. Artichokes are in fact a very large thistle. Smaller thistles are
like artichokes, including in taste, though eating the flower heads, the commonly eaten part of artichokes, would be very labor intensive and probably
not worth the trouble. However, the leaves and stalks of many thistles do
have that same pleasant soft, sweet flavor. There are at least seven true thistles
of the genus *Cirsium* and many other thistle plants, including milk thistle
(*Silybum marianum*), in the High Sierra. They are all edible, but some are
very bitter—just sample them and see which ones taste good. Thistles are
not only tasty but also very nutritious. Truman Everts, who in 1870 got lost
in the wilderness that would become Yellowstone National Park, ate thistle
roots for thirty-seven days to keep from starving as he made his way down the
Yellowstone River back to his companions.

Identification: Thistles are low-
growing flowering plants up to three
feet high, with sharp, usually serrated
leaves that have spikes on the edges.
The protective prickles also often
cover the stem. The flower head is
showy with a purple flower on top.
Thistles are biennial, meaning that
they create a basal rosette of leaves
the first year and then shoot up a
flower stalk the second.

Where to Find: Find thistles in
disturbed places, at road edges, in
meadows, and in sunny spots.

When to Harvest: Harvest thistles in
spring and summer.

How to Harvest: Harvest by simply
cutting off the desired part.

Poisonous Look-Alikes: There are
none to my knowledge. Some wild
lettuces look like thistles, though

with smoother leaves and fewer
spikes. They are barely palatable, but
they are not poisonous.

Edible and Useful Parts

Leaves: Cut off the spikes on the
outer edges of the leaf. Eat the leaves
raw or cooked.

Flowers: These are usually too
covered in spikes to eat, but can be
eaten when very young; just steam or
boil them.

Seeds: You can roast the seeds and
grind them into flour.

Stalks: Thistle stalks are delicious.
Harvest them in spring when they
are young and tender. Cut off
the stalk and simply peel off the
outer spiky layer with a knife. Eat
like asparagus raw or cooked. If
dethorned, thistle stalks can be used
as hand drills for fire making.

Roots: The root is medicinal and very nutritious. It can be eaten raw or cooked.

Other uses: Thistledown is good tinder or filling.

Thistles are high in fiber, vitamin C, calcium, iron, and potassium. They also have many medicinal uses.

Thistles are common and often considered a problematic weed.

Spring Thistle Stalk Sauté

This is a fun side dish. Serve it at dinner. Your family or guests will think it's delicious and have a hard time guessing what they're eating.

Ingredients
- 20 thistle stalks, washed, peeled, and cut
- Butter
- Garlic, minced

Heat the butter and minced garlic on a skillet. Throw in the thistle stalks and sauté for 5 minutes. Serve with pasta or potatoes, on a pizza, or by themselves.

WEST COAST GOLDENROD

Solidago elongata
Asteraceae (Other common edible species in this family—daisies,
   artichokes, dandelions, thistles, sunflowers)
Originates in the western United States

Goldenrod is such a showy plant that I was surprised to find out it's edible. It turns out that this tall, yellow-flowered plant that I see all the time in the meadows is nutritious, tasty, and medicinal as well. Its height and color make it easy to find—I often notice it from afar even while zooming by on my bike rides near the lake—and it can last late into the summer. Goldenrod needs to be cooked, but it is still fairly easy to grab some flowers and add them to a soup or stir-fry.

Identification: West Coast goldenrod is a tall, slender plant up to five feet tall. Leaves are lanceolate and thin, with very lightly jagged edges. The stem is a little bit hairy, almost spiked. The flowers are tiny, but there are many of them, and they grow in a showy cluster at the top of the stem.

Where to Find: Goldenrod grows in meadows, clearings, and ditches.

When to Harvest: Harvest goldenrod in spring, summer, and sometimes early fall.

How to Harvest: Just pinch off the desired part carefully.

Poisonous Look-Alikes: Some plants of the *Senecio* and *Packera* genera may look like goldenrod. Despite its name, butterweed (*Packera glabella*), for example, is toxic. When new to eating goldenrod, it's best to wait until it flowers to identify it with certainty. Goldenrod flowers are very small and in abundant clusters.

Caution: Raw goldenrod may be toxic, so it's best to cook it.

Edible and Useful Parts

Leaves: The leaves can be used fried, steamed, or boiled. They can also be dried for tea. They are best harvested when young, right before the plant blooms.

Flowers: The flowers can be used as a flavoring in dishes, or dried and used as tea or added to flour. They can be added to a variety of dishes, from eggs to cake to soup to cordials.

Stems: The stems are best harvested early in the season. Peel them and roast them in the oven.

Benefits: The health benefits of goldenrod are extensive. Herbalists use it to help with the function of many human systems, including the kidneys and bladder.

Sustainability: Goldenrod is usually very common.

Goldenrod Eggs with Goldenrod

There is a common recipe called Goldenrod Eggs. I thought it would be fun to add a bit of actual goldenrod to it.

Ingredients
- 2 hard-boiled eggs
- 2 tablespoons flour
- 5 tablespoons butter
- 1 cup milk
- ½ cup goldenrod flowers, washed and finely chopped
- Salt and pepper to taste

Cut the eggs in half and separate the yolks. Chop up the egg whites. In a saucepan, fry the goldenrod flowers in the butter. Add in the milk, flour, salt, and pepper. Stir in the egg whites until just mixed in. Push the egg yolks through a sieve and sprinkle them over the sauce. Serve with toast.

WESTERN BLUE FLAX

Linum lewisii
Linaceae
Originates in western North America and Alaska

———

One of my favorite spots to hike is close to the Truckee airport. It is a gorgeous meadow where there is a rich history of human habitation dating back tens of thousands of years. Going there in wildflower season is a treat, with yellow tarweed everywhere and blue flax flowers waving in the wind against a landscape of gentle mountain ridges. Flax is perhaps not the most commonly recognized wild edible, as the edible part is its seeds. However, the seeds are so good for you and easy to harvest that they are good to know about. They are not edible raw, however. Western blue flax is also known as Lewis' flax and blue flax.

Identification: Western blue flax is a gentle annual low-growing plant that sometimes reaches a height of two to three feet. It has a slender stem and a beautiful lilac-blue flower. Flax often grows in bunches, though can sometimes be seen alone. The light grayish green leaves don't have stalks and are slender and oval shaped. The flowers have five petals and a yellow center. The seedpods are round and form en masse at the top. The seeds are brownish black and slippery. The seeds become slimy when wet.

Where to Find: Western blue flax grows in dry sunny meadows and on rocky slopes.

When to Harvest: This plant can be harvested in mid- to late summer.

How to Harvest: Wait until the seedpods are dry and collect them in the field. Alternatively, cut some stems and bunch them to dry at home; when they are fully dry, crush or shake the seeds out.

Poisonous Look-Alikes: Although I can't think of a poisonous look-alike, there are many blue-flowered plants in the Sierra that are not edible. It can be hard to identify flax when in seed, so it is a good idea to get to know it while it is flowering.

Caution: The seeds are only edible roasted or cooked, as they contain cyanide.

Edible and Useful Parts

Seeds: The seeds are edible when roasted and have a nice soft nutty flavor. They can be used in baked goods or sprinkled on cereals. They are also often made into oil.

Other uses: Flax makes a nice fiber for fabric and cordage. The word *linen* comes from the genus name (*Linum*), as linen is made from the stems of flax and in the past was used for fabric more often than cotton.

Benefits: Flax seeds are high in heart-healthy omega oils. They can also be used as a laxative. Flaxseeds need to be ground for maximum health benefits.

Sustainability: Flax is a precious wildflower. I recommend that you harvest only a few seeds in the wild and cultivate them in your yard for harvesting. Otherwise, preserve the wild plants by only harvesting a bit to taste.

Wild Flax Trail Bars

This recipe can accommodate any wild seeds and nuts you have, as well as dried wild berries and fruit.

Ingredients

- 1 cup oats
- 1 tablespoon flax seeds, roasted and ground
- 1 tablespoon dock seeds, roasted and ground
- ¾ cup total of your choice of nuts, sunflower seeds, or other seeds
- ¾ cup total of your choice of raisins, date pieces, dried apricot pieces, small dried fruit pieces, dried rose hips, wild currants, etc.
- 1 cup puffed healthy cereal or amaranth
- ¼ cup honey
- ¼ cup turbinado sugar
- 1 teaspoon vanilla
- Pinch of cinnamon
- ¼ cup almond butter, peanut butter, or sunflower butter
- Pinch of salt

Toast oats, nuts, and seeds for a minute while stirring in a frying pan. Add dried fruit and puffed cereal and toss in a large bowl. Combine almond or other butter, honey, sugar, and vanilla in a saucepan and cook at low heat just until it bubbles. Pour into the dry ingredients and mix. Pour onto a lined or oiled pan and press down with oiled hands. Refrigerate for an hour and cut into desired shapes. Take these bars with you on your next foraging expedition.

WILD CURRANTS

Ribes spp.

Grossulariaceae (Other common edible species in this
family—gooseberries)

Originate on the West Coast of North America; cultivated species
originate in Europe

I love seeing the currants blossom in the Sierra. The abundant pink and
yellow blossoms signal the coming of spring. I grew up with the much larger
black and red currants of Finland and have fond memories of picking them
for my grandmother to make juice out of; it would last us all winter and was
a bit of a cure-all for any cold or ailment. I still love the somewhat pungent
smell of currant leaves. These California currants are much smaller and less
juicy than their European cousins, but they are still tasty. There are three main
species of currant in the Sierra, wax currant (*R. cereum*), sticky currant (*R.
viscosissimum*), and mountain pink currant (*R. nevadense*); they range in color
and taste. All species are edible, as far as I know, but some are less palatable.
Sample the ones you find and see whether you like them.

Identification: Wild currants grow
as shrubs up to six feet high. The
leaves are reminiscent of a soft maple
leaf and have a strong aroma when
crushed, sometimes smelling good,
like citrus, sometimes not so good.
The pink, yellow, or red flowers cas-
cade down in clumps and ripen into
red, golden, or purple berries that
look like mini grapes.

Where to Find: Wild currants grow in
forests, at forest edges, and in clearings; find it in partial shade or sun.

When to Harvest: Harvest wild currants in spring and summer.

How to Harvest: Harvest by pinching
off the leaves, flowers, or berries.

Poisonous Look-Alikes: There are
none with a similar leaf.

Edible and Useful Parts

Flowers: You can use the flowers as
decoration on cakes or salads or as a
flavoring in drinks.

Leaves: You can dry these for tea or
use fresh as wraps; some say wilted
currant leaves of some species can
be toxic.

Berries: The berries can be eaten raw
as is or cooked into pies, jellies, or
juices. Because California currants
tend to be dry, I let them dry and
use them in baked goods. They get
sweeter when dried as well.

Benefits: Currants are high in vitamin C and many minerals.

Sustainability: Currants are common
in the Sierra, but the berries are not
always abundant, so harvest in moderation. I have not seen wildlife eat
very many of them for some reason,
and many berries rot or dry on the
bush, which to me indicates that it is
OK to harvest a few.

Wild Currant Scones

Wild currants are a bit small and seedy for most recipes, but are a fun addition to scones.

Ingredients
- 2 cups flour
- 1 tablespoon baking powder
- 2 tablespoons maple syrup
- Pinch of salt
- ½ stick butter or vegan butter
- 2 eggs or egg replacer
- ½ cup cream or high-fat nondairy milk
- ½ cup dried wild currants or a mixture of wild berries

Preheat oven to 400°. Combine dry ingredients in a medium-size bowl. Cut in the cold butter until it forms a crumbly dough. Stir in the cream, eggs, and then currants. Make a lump out of the dough and roll it onto a floured surface. Cut it into triangular pieces and place on a greased baking sheet. Brush with egg white if desired. Bake for 15 minutes until golden brown.

WILD ONIONS

Allium spp.
Alliaceae (Other common edible species in this family—garlic)
Originate in various places, including California

—

I have yet to find an abundant onion-harvesting spot in the High Sierra. I have of course found onions, but from the forager's viewpoint, there are two types. There are those that grow alone in dry areas, which I do not harvest, as there are not many, and they are more of a beautiful wildflower than a food source. Common examples of these in the High Sierra are Sierra onion (*A. campanulatum*) and pink-star onion (*A. platycaule*). Then there are those that grow in wet areas in abundance. Those are the ones I would like to harvest; swamp onion is the common variety of these in the Sierra. I have found plenty of the dry-land type on my High Sierra hikes, but not yet the second type. That is just fine with me, as part of the fun of foraging is the search. Foraging is like a wild treasure hunt. So I will keep looking and will probably happen upon a meadow of wild onions someday. Wild onions are indeed onions. They are most similar to chives or small leeks. You can use the greens and bulb, as with green onions or ramps.

Identification: Wild onions are low-growing plants with long, grass-like leaves that are often leathery in texture. Their flowers range from white to purple and grow in clusters that in some cases can form a small ball shape. The bulbs are small and white. The whole plant smells like onion or garlic.

Where to Find: Wild onions grow in a variety of habitats, including dry slopes and wet meadow areas.

When to Harvest: Harvest these plants in summer.

How to Harvest: Pinch off some leaves or dig out the bulb.

Poisonous Look-Alikes: Onions can look very similar to death camas or star lily, so make sure the plant smells clearly like onion.

Edible and Useful Parts

Leaves: These can be eaten cooked or raw. Use them as you would chives or leeks in a recipe.

Flowers: Use the flowers for decoration on savory dishes or salads.

Bulbs: The bulbs can be eaten cooked or raw. Some are very strong in flavor, more like garlic, others mild. They can be used as you would leeks.

Benefits: Wild onions are rich in vitamins A and C.

Sustainability: I would not harvest from the single onions growing on the hillsides. Perhaps if there were several, I might sample a bit of leaf. In some places, though, there is an abundance of wild onions, in which case harvesting them is just fine.

There's really no need to remove the bulb most of the time; just harvesting some leaves will allow the plant to keep living. You can also plant wild onions in your garden.

Wild Onion and Potato Soup

This is an quick and easy-to-make soup, and if you don't have enough wild onions, you can increase the amount of garlic or store-bought onion you use in this recipe.

Ingredients
- Bunch of wild onions, washed and chopped
- 1 onion, chopped
- 1 clove garlic, minced
- 3 potatoes, washed and diced
- 3 cups broth of your choice
- 2 tablespoons. butter
- Salt and pepper to taste

Fry the onions and garlic in butter. Add the rest of the ingredients and bring to a boil. Reduce heat and simmer for 30 minutes or until potatoes are soft. Let cool a bit and use an immersion blender to create a uniform consistency. Garnish with wild onion greens or flowers. Serve with wild-seed crackers, such as dock crackers.

WILD PLUMS AND CHERRIES

Prunus spp.

Rosaceae (Other common edible species in this family—roses, apples, strawberries, raspberries)

Originate in various places and the West Coast of the United States

—

Wild plums in the High Sierra can either be feral—trees that have escaped from gardens and become naturalized—or native species such as choke cherry. Some are sweet enough to be eaten raw; others are very sour and are best cooked. All edible sweet fruit is good news to the forager, and because these are fruit on the tree and many people don't know about them, they can be quite abundant when you find them. They are small, however, usually at most the size of store-bought cherries, and therefore require some processing. I have provided some time-saving tips later in this section. The plums and cherries you can find in the High Sierra are Western chokecherry (*P. virginiana*), bitter cherry (*P. emarginata*), and Sierra plum (*P. subcordata*), as well as some naturalized garden varieties, as I mentioned earlier.

Identification: Plum and cherry are small trees or shrubs with ovate leaves and dark-red to purple fruit. They have white or pink usually five-petaled flowers that flower profusely in the spring.

Where to Find: You can find plum and cherry trees in sunny and moist areas.

When to Harvest: The fruit is ripe in the summer.

How to Harvest: Pick the fruit off the tree when fully ripe.

Poisonous Look-Alikes: Other nonedible berries might resemble them, but wild plums and cherries have large pits and are moist and fleshy.

Caution: Cherries and plums contain cyanide in the pits, leaves, and wood; those parts should be removed before eating.

Edible and Useful Parts

Fruit: The ripe fruit can be eaten raw or cooked. Some varieties are too astringent to eat raw, but turn sweet when cooked.

Benefits: Wild plums and cherries are high in vitamins C and B6, potassium, and magnesium.

Sustainability: Wild cherries and plums range in abundance. Many of them are feral and fine to forage. If you find an isolated shrub in a wilder area, it might be better just to sample a few, whereas a stand of trees can provide a rich harvest.

Wild Fruit Leather

This is an easy way to use wild plum and cherry pulp. It's easiest to prepare if you have a dehydrator, but you can also do it in an oven.

Ingredients
- 6 cups wild plums
- Sweetener if desired
- Water

Bring the plums and water to a boil. Let simmer until the pits separate from the fruit. Strain through a large sieve. Discard the pits. Spread the pulp on dehydrator sheets or baking sheeets. Follow the dehydrator's directions, or bake at 150° for 5–6 hrs. Let cool and cut into strips. Well sealed, the fruit leather can be stored for up to a year.

YAMPAHS

Perideridia spp.

Apiaceae (Other common edible species in this family—carrots, dill, parsley)

Originate in Central and Northern California

—

Yampah is one of the rare wild edibles that actually has a starchy tuberous root that can be a filling meal rather than just a light snack. This makes it a very valuable find for the forager or survivalist. It is a close relative of poison hemlock, however, and to the untrained eye, yampah resembles poison hemlock when young, so I suggest not harvesting it until you've carefully learned to identify it. There are three species of yampah in the High Sierra: Bolander's yampah (*P. bolanderi*), Lemmon's yampah (*P. lemmonii*), and Parish's yampah (*P. parishii*). All can be used similarly.

Identification: Yampah is a low-growing plant with a slender stalk up to two feet high. The leaves are slender and come off of a thin leaf stalk to form a shape similar to a very sparse carrot leaf. The flowers grow in clusters on small stalks, making them umbel shaped. The tiny yampah flowers are sparse, with green centers. The tubers are one to two inches long; they are white and have slits in them often covered in brown.

Where to Find: Yampah grows in moist meadows and open forests.

When to Harvest: Harvest this plant in spring and summer.

How to Harvest: Pinch off the leaves and flowers. Dig out the tubers carefully.

Poisonous Look-Alikes: Poison hemlock, which is deadly, can be mistaken for yampah. You want to know the differences very clearly. If in doubt, wait until the yampah flowers, even though the tubers are better before. The individual flowers of yampah are bigger than poison hemlock flowers, which are tiny but in larger clusters. The leaves of yampah are also much more sparse. The poison hemlock stalk sometimes has red or purple dots on it, but not always. Yampah can also be confused with water hemlock, which is also deadly, if it's growing near water. Water hemlock leaves are more substantial than yampah leaves.

Edible and Useful Parts

Leaves and flowers: These can be eaten raw or cooked.

Tubers: The tubers are delicious cooked or raw, much like a small carrot but more nutty.

Benefits: The tubers are rich in carbohydrates.

Sustainability: Yampah has been becoming increasingly uncommon. I include it here because of its important history as a common wild-edible plant. At this time, however, I would recommend planting it in your own garden for easier identification and greater abundance.

YARROW

Achillea millefolium
Asteraceae (Other common edible species in this family—daisies,
  artichokes, dandelions, thistles, sunflowers)
Originates in Asia, North America, and Europe

——

Yarrow is one of the first plants that appears in the spring in the High Sierra and starts flowering quite early. In other places, it never looked very edible to me, but in the Sierra the bunches of leaves look quite delicious. It has a spicy flavor that can be a bit of an acquired taste. Yarrow is an age-old medicinal plant particularly known for stopping bleeding and curing fevers. The name *Achillea* refers to Achilles, the invincible Greek warrior with his famously vulnerable heel. Yarrow was carried by soldiers because of its healing properties. Because of its potent taste that is a bit minty or fresh, sage-like but also pungent and bitter, yarrow can add an interesting flavor as a spice or an ingredient in a salad.

Identification: Yarrow is a herbaceous plant up to three feet tall, but rarely that. Its leaves have numerous little pieces and look almost like soft green feathers. The flowers grow in abundant clusters with flat tops and are usually white, but can also be pink. The whole plant smells good, a bit pungent and green.

Where to Find: You can find this plant in moist places, meadows, and snowmelt areas.

When to Harvest: Harvest yarrow in spring and summer.

How to Harvest: Just cut off a flower or leaf sprig.

Poisonous Look-Alikes: Poison hemlock could look similar with its white flowers and leaf shape. Yarrow smells aromatic, though; the leaves are more fuzzy and feathery, and its flowers look like flowers with petals rather than indistinct clusters.

Edible and Useful Parts

Leaves: Young or dried leaves can be used as a spice or a flavoring ingredient in small amounts. The younger the leaves, the better. They work well in salads or with meat, fish, or other herbs. The leaves can even work in sweet desserts such as ice cream. Yarrow is best used fresh, not cooked, and in very small amounts. It's a better garnish than an addition to a meal because it can be very bitter when cooked. It's very potent.

Flowers: These can be used for decoration and as a spice.

Benefits: Yarrow is rich in many minerals and vitamin C.

Sustainability: Yarrow is very common in the Sierra, and it's unlikely you would want to use it in large amounts.

Yarrow Tortillas

Homemade tortillas are great in general, and with yarrow these have a bit of spice and can be great as a fish taco wrap. I got the idea from a foraging blog.

Ingredients
- 2½ cups masa harina
- 1½ cups room-temperature water
- 2 sprigs of young yarrow leaves, finely chopped
- Pinch of salt

In a bowl, mix the yarrow into the masa harina. Pour in the water and quickly mix. Roll the dough into equal-size balls. Flatten each ball and roll out with a rolling pin. Cook in an ungreased frying pan on medium heat for a few minutes on each side. Serve with your favorite tortilla toppings.

Next Steps

I hope this book has inspired you to learn more about wild edible plants and get out there and sample some. Here are some suggestions for how to continue your learning journey:

- Get to know the most poisonous plants first so you do not make any mistakes. Make sure you can identify poison and water hemlocks.

- Join a local wild food walk. (I often offer them. Check out my website, www.miaandler.com.)

- Look at foraging videos for some of these plants on the internet.

- Join a wild-food CSA if there is one in your area, and support your local foragers.

- Find a foraging buddy who can join you in looking for useful plants; we often stay more motivated when we have company.

- Download an app such as iSeek. It will help you identify new plants, but remember that these apps are not perfect: you should always confirm with several sources before eating a plant based on an app's identification.

- Just go outside and start noticing plants. Walk a bit more slowly or perhaps take plant breaks on exercise outings.

- Get to know a certain plant well and use it in a recipe. There's no need to get to know all plants right away.

Enjoy your foraging adventures!

The Plants by Season and Index of Plant Names

Plant Name	Scientific Name	Fall	Winter	Spring	Summer	Page
Alders	*Alnus* spp.	X	X	X	X	19
American brooklime/ American speedwell	*Veronica americana*	X		X	X	17
Aspen	*Populus tremuloides*	X	X	X	X	19
Birches	*Betula occidentalis* and *Betula pendula*	X	X	X	X	19
Bittercresses	*Cardamine* spp.			X		101
Blackberries	*Rubus* spp.	X		X	X	23
Blue dicks	*Dichelostemma congestum*			X	X	27
Brodiaeas	*Brodiaea* spp.			X	X	27
Bush chinquapin	*Chrysolepis sempervirens*	X			X	31
Cattails	*Typha* spp.	X	X	X	X	33
Cinquefoils	*Potentilla* spp.			X	X	37
Cleavers/bedstraws	*Galium* spp.			X	X	39
Clovers	*Trifolium* spp.	X		X	X	43
Common camas lily	*Camassia quamash*			X	X	45
Cow parsnip	*Heracleum maximum*	X		X	X	49
Crab apples	*Peraphyllum ramosissimum, Malus* spp.	X				51
Currants	*Ribes* spp.	X		X	X	169
Dandelion	*Taraxacum officinale*			X	X	55
Docks	*Rumex* spp.	X	X	X	X	59

Plant Name	Scientific Name	Fall	Winter	Spring	Summer	Page
Douglas fir	*Pseudotsuga menziesii*	X	X	X	X	114
Elderberries	*Sambucus* spp.	X			X	61
Ferns	*Polypodiaceae* spp.			X		65
Fireweed	*Chamerion angustifolium*			X	X	69
Gooseberries	*Ribes* spp.	X		X	X	141
Hedge mustards	*Sisymbrium* spp.	X		X	X	101
Horsetails	*Equisetum* spp.	X		X	X	71
Incense cedar	*Calocedrus decurrens*	X	X	X	X	75
Junipers	*Juniperus* spp.	X	X	X	X	77
Lamb's quarters	*Chenopodium* spp.	X			X	81
Manzanitas	*Arctostaphylos* spp.	X		X	X	83
Milk thistle	*Silybum marianum*	X		X	X	161
Miner's lettuce	*Claytonia perfoliate*			X		143
Monardellas and pennyroyal	*Monardella* spp.			X	X	91
Mountain ash (rowan)	*Sorbus* spp.	X			X	89
Mountain coyote mint	*Monardella odoratissima*	X		X	X	91
Mugwort	*Artemisia douglasiana*	x		X	X	95
Mullein	*Verbascum thapsus*			X	X	97
Mustards	*Brassica* spp.			X	X	101
Oregon grape/barberry	*Berberis aquifolium*	X		X	X	103
Peppergrass	*Lepidium virginicum*			X		101
Pineapple weed	*Matricaria discoidea*			X	X	107
Pines	*Pinus* spp.	X	X	X	X	109
Plantains	*Plantago* spp.	X		X	X	117

Plant Name	Scientific Name	Fall	Winter	Spring	Summer	Page
Purslane	*Portulaca oleracea*	X		X	X	119
Raspberries	*Rubus* spp.	X		X	X	23
Roses	*Rosa* spp.	X	X	X	X	125
Sage	*Salvia pachypylla*	X		X	X	127
Sagebrush	*Artemisia* spp.	X		X	X	127
Salsify	*Tragopogon dubious*			X	X	131
Serviceberries	*Amelanchier* spp.	X			X	137
Shepherd's purse	*Capsella bursa-pastors*			X	X	101
Spring beauties	*Claytonia* spp.			X	X	143
Stinging nettle	*Urtica dioica*			X	X	147
Strawberries	*Fragaria* spp.			X	X	153
Tarweeds	*Madia* spp.	X			X	155
Thimbleberry	*Rubus parviflorus*			X	X	157
Thistles	*Cirsium* spp.			X	X	161
True firs	*Abies* spp.	X	X	X	X	109
Watercress	*Nasturtium officinale*	X		X	X	101
West Coast goldenrod	*Solidago elongata*			X	X	163
Western blue flax	*Linum lewisii*	X				167
Wild onions	*Allium* spp.			X	X	173
Wild plums and cherries	*Prunus* spp.		X		X	175
Wild radish	*Raphanus sativus*			X	X	101
Yampahs	*Perideridia* spp.			X	X	179
Yarrow	*Achillea millefolium*	X		X	X	181

Additional Edible Plants in the High Sierra

This book focuses on the most delicious and available edible plants in the High Sierra. There are certainly other edible plants in the area, but I haven't included them in the book because they are not common in the High Sierra, are only marginally edible, or need to be protected and so should not be collected. They are listed here for curious readers.

Plant Name	Scientific Name
Alpine mountain sorrel	*Oxyria digyna*
Alpine wintergreen	*Gaultheria humifusa*
Alumroots	*Heuchera* spp.
American bistort	*Bistorta bistortoides*
Anderson thorn bush	*Lycium andersonii*
Arrowleaf balsamroot	*Balsamhoriza sagittata*
Bee plant	*Cleome serrulata*
Bellflowers	*Campanula* spp.
Bitterroot	*Lewisia rediviva*
Bluebell	*Mertensia ciliata*
Bog bilberry	*Vaccinium uliginosum*
Bulrushes	*Typha* spp.
California Indian potato	*Orogenia fusiformis*
California nutmeg	*Torreya californica*
California valerian	*Valeriana californica*
Chickweed	*Stellaria media*
Clarkias	*Clarkia* spp.
Common self-heal	*Prunella vulgaris*
Flat sedge/nutgrass	*Cyperus eragrostis*
Fritillaries	*Fritillaria* spp.

Plant Name	Scientific Name
Giant blazing star	*Mentzelia laevicaulis*
Giant hyssop	*Agastache urticifolia*
Gray's lovage	*Ligusticum grayi*
Hazelnut	*Corylus cornuta*
Holodiscus	*Holodiscus microphyllus*
Lomatiums	*Lomatium* spp.
Maples	*Acer* spp.
Mare's-tail	*Hippuris vulgaris*
Mariposa lilies and star tulips	*Calochortus* spp.
Monkeyflowers	*Mimulus* spp.
Mountain hemlock	*Tsuga mertensiana*
Netleaf hackberry	*Celtis reticulata*
Oaks	*Quercus* spp. and *Lithocarpus densiflora*
Osoberry	*Oemleria cerasiformis*
Pigweed, amaranth	*Amaranthus* spp.
Quaking aspen	*Populus tremuloides*
Redmaids	*Calandrinia ciliata*
Redstem stork's-bill	*Erodium cicutarium*
Rocky pteryxia	*Cymopterus terebinthinus*
Saltbush	*Atriplex* spp.
Saxifrages	*Saxifraga* spp.
Sedges	*Carex* spp.
Sierra sweet bay	*Myrica hartwegii*
Skunkbush	*Rhus trilobata*
Soaproots	*Chlorogalum* spp.
Stonecrop	*Sedum* spp.
Toyon	*Heteromeles arbutifolia*
Tule-potato	*Sagittaria cuneata*

Plant Name	Scientific Name
Twisted stalk	*Streptopus amplexifolius*
Violets	*Viola* spp.
Watershield	*Brasenia schreberi*
Waxy checkerbloom	*Sidalcea glaucesens*
White bog orchid	*Platanthera dilatata*
Wild geraniums	*Geranium* spp.
Wild ginger	*Asarum hartwegii* and *Asarum lemmonii*
Wild licorice	*Glychyrriza lepidota*
Wintercress	*Barbarea orthoceras*
Wood sorrels	*Oxalis* spp.
Yerba santa	*Eriodictyon californicum*

Resources

Kane, Charles W. *Wild Edible Plants of Nevada*. Dallas, TX: Lincoln Press, 2021.

Redbud Chapter, California Native Plant Society. *Wildflowers of Nevada and Placer Counties, California*, 2nd ed. Sacramento: Redbud Chapter and CNPS Press, 2017.

Vizgirdas, Ray S., and Rey-Vizgirdas, Edna M. *Wild Plants of the Sierra Nevada*. Reno: University of Nevada Press, 1960.

Weeden, Norman F. *A Sierra Nevada Flora*. Berkeley, CA: Wilderness Press, 1996.

About the Author

Mia Andler is committed to facilitating meaningful connection to nature. She is the coauthor of *The Bay Area Forager* and has been backpacking and foraging in the Sierra Nevada for over twenty-five years. She is also the founder and executive director of Vilda, a 501c(3) nonprofit that runs nature connection programs for children in Tahoe, Truckee, and the San Francisco Bay Area. She has been foraging since she was a little girl and has studied the regenerative practices of earth-based cultures around the world. Mia has appeared on television, film, and radio. She lives with her children in Truckee, California.